**FAZIL
ISKANDER**

THE THIRTEENTH LABOUR
OF HERCULES

Stories

Translated by *Robert Daglish* and *K. M. Cook-Horujy*

Raduga Publishers Moscow

Translation from the Russian
Designed by *Andrei Nikulin*

First printing 1978
Second printing 1989

English translation © Progress Publishers 1978
© Raduga Publishers 1989

Printed in the Union of Soviet Socialist Republics

ISBN 5-05-002444-7

CONTENTS*

* These stories were translated by Robert Daglish with the exception
of *The Letter* which was translated by K. M. Cook-Horujy.

The Thirteenth Labour of Hercules

stories

SOMETHING ABOUT MYSELF

Let's just talk. Let's talk about things we don't have to talk about, pleasant things. Let's talk about some of the amusing sides of human nature, as embodied in people we know. There is nothing more enjoyable than discussing certain odd habits of our acquaintances. Because, you see, talking about them makes us aware of our own healthy normality. It implies that we, too, could indulge in such idiosyncrasies if we liked, but we don't like because we have no use for them. Or have we?

One of the rather amusing features of human nature is that each of us tries to live up to an image imposed upon him by other people.

Now here is an example from my own experience.

When I was at school the whole form was one day given the task of turning a patch of seaside wasteland into a place of cultured rest and recreation. Strange though it may seem, we actually succeeded.

We planted out the patch with eucalyptus seedlings, using the cluster method, which was an advanced method for those times. Admittedly, when there were not many seedlings and too much wasteland left, we began to put only one seedling in each hole, thus giving the new, progressive method and the old method the chance to show their worth in free competition.

In a few years a beautiful grove of eucalyptus trees grew up on that wasteland and it was quite impossible to tell where the clusters and where the single seedlings had been. Then it was said that the single seedlings, being in direct proximity to the clusters and envying them with a thoroughly good sort of envy, had made an effort and caught up.

Be that as it may, when I come back to my hometown

nowadays, I sometimes take it easy in the shade of those now enormous trees and feel like a sentimental patriarch. Eucalyptus grows very fast, so anyone who wants to feel like a sentimental patriarch can plant an eucalyptus tree and live to see its crown towering high above him, its leaves tinkling in the breeze like the toys on a New Year tree.

But that's not the point. The point is that on that far-off day when we were reclaiming the wasteland one of the boys drew attention to the way I held the stretcher we were using for carrying soil. The P. T. instructor in charge of us also noticed the way I held the stretcher. Everyone noticed the way I held the stretcher. Some pretext for amusement had to be found and found it was. It turned out that I was holding the stretcher like an Inveterate Idler.

This was the first crystal to form and it started a vigorous process of crystallisation which I did all I could to assist, so as to become finally crystallised in the preordained direction.

Now everything contributed to the building of my image. If I sat through a mathematics test not troubling anyone and calmly waiting for my neighbour to solve the problem, everyone attributed this not to my stupidity but to sheer idleness. Naturally I made no attempt to disillusion them. When for Russian composition I would write something straight out of my head without looking anything up in textbooks and cribs, this was taken as even more convincing proof of my incorrigible idleness.

In order to preserve my image I deliberately neglected my duties as monitor. Everyone soon became so used to this that when any other member of the form forgot to perform his monitorial duties, the teacher, with the whole form voicing its approval in the background, would make me wipe the blackboard or carry the physics apparatus into the room.

Further development of my image compelled me to give up homework. But to maintain the suspense of the situation I had to show reasonable results in my schoolwork. So every day, as soon as instruction in the humanitarian subjects began, I would lean forward on my desk and pretend to be dozing. If the teacher protested, I would say I was ill but did not want to miss the lesson, so as not to get left behind. In this reclining attitude I would listen attentively to what the teacher was saying without being diverted by any of the usual pranks, and try to remember everything he told us. After a lesson on any new material, if there was still some time left, I would volunteer to answer questions in advance, for the next lesson.

The teachers liked this because it flattered their pedagogical vanity. It meant that they could explain their subject so well and so clearly that the pupils were able to take it all in without even referring to the textbooks.

The teacher would put down a good mark for me in the register, the bell would ring and everyone would be satisfied. And nobody but I ever realised that the information I had just memorised was about to romp out of my head just as the bar romps out of the hands of the weightlifter the moment he hears the umpire's approving "Up!"

To be perfectly accurate, I had better add that sometimes, when reclining on my desk pretending to doze, I would actually fall into a doze, though I could still hear the voice of the teacher. Much later on I discovered that some people use the same, or almost the same, method for learning languages. I believe it would not appear too immodest if I were to say that I am the inventor of this method. I make no mention of the occasions when I actually fell asleep because they were rare.

After a while rumours concerning this Inveterate Idler reached the ears of our headmaster and for some reason he decided that it was I who had taken the telescope that had disappeared six months ago from the geography room. I don't know why he drew this conclusion. Possibly he reasoned that the very idea of even a visual reduction of distance would appeal most of all to a victim of sloth. I cannot think of any other explanation. Luckily, the telescope was recovered soon afterwards, but from then on people kept an eye on me, as if I might get up to some trick at any moment.

It soon turned out, however, that I had no such intentions, and that, on the contrary, I was a very obedient and conscientious slacker. What was more, slacker though I was, I seemed to be getting quite decent results.

Then they decided to apply to me a method of concentrated education that was fashionable in those years. The essence of this method was that all the teachers in the school taking advantage of his confusion, turn him into a shining example of scholastic attainment.

It was assumed that other backward pupils, envying him with a thoroughly Good Envy, would make an effort to rise to his level. Just like the singly planted eucalyptus seedlings.

The effect of the method depended on the suddenness of the mass attack. Otherwise the pupil might succeed in slipping out of range or actually discredit the method itself.

As a rule the experiment achieved its purpose. Before the hurly-burly caused by the mass attack could disperse, the reformed pupil would take his place with the best in the class, impudently wearing the smile of a despoiled virgin.

When this happened, the teachers, envying one another with perhaps not quite such a Good Envy, would zealously follow his progress in their markbook, and, of course, each teacher would try to ensure that the victorious upward curve of scholastic attainment was not broken within the limits of his subject.

Well, either they piled into me too enthusiastically, or else they forgot what my own fairly respectable level had been before they started but when they began to analyse the results of their experiment it turned out that they had trained me up to the level of a potential medal-winner.

"You could pull off a silver," my form-mistress announced rather dazedly.

The potential medal-winners were a small ambitious caste of untouchables. Even the teachers were somewhat afraid of them. They were to become the honour of the school, and to damage the reputation of a potential medal-winner was equivalent to threatening the honour of the school. Every potential medal-winner had at some

11

time by his own efforts achieved distinction in one of the basic subjects and had then been coached to the necessary degree of perfection in all the rest.

So, with my school diploma sewn into my jacket pocket together with my money I got into a train and set off for Moscow. At that time the train journey from Abkhazia to Moscow took three days. I had plenty of time to think things over, and of all the possible variants for my future education I chose the philosophical faculty of the university. My choice may have been decided by the following circumstance.

About two years before this I had exchanged some books with a friend of mine. I had given him Conan Doyle's *The Adventures of Sherlock Holmes*, and he had given me an odd volume of Hegel's *Lectures on Aesthetics*. I had already been told that Hegel was simultaneously both a philosopher and a genius and that, in those far-off years, was a strong enough recommendation for me.

Since I had not yet heard that Hegel was a difficult author to read, I understood nearly everything I read. If I came across a paragraph with long, incomprehensible words, I simply skipped it because the meaning was clear enough without it. Later on, when studying at the institute, I learned that besides their rational kernel the works of Hegel contained quite a lot of idealistic husk. I guessed that just those paragraphs I had skipped were the husk. My way of reading him had been to open the book at some verse quotation from Schiller or Goethe, and then read round it, trying to keep as near to the quotation as possible, like a camel on the edge of an oasis. Some of Hegel's thoughts surprised me by their high probability of truth. For instance, he called the fable a servile genre, which sounded true enough, and I made a point of remembering this so as to avoid that genre in the future.

Eventually, for some unknown reason I gave up reading that volume. Perhaps I had used up all the quotations or perhaps it was something else. I decided that I had far too much time ahead of me and that one day I would read all the volumes in their proper order. But I still haven't started on them.

It may well be that this random reading of mine

and also a certain lack of clarity in the actions of mankind on the road to a bright future were responsible for my choice of the philosophical faculty.

In Moscow, after certain adventures that I shall not relate because I need them as plots for my stories, I entered not the university but the Library Institute. When I had been studying there for three years, it dawned on me that it would be more interesting and more profitable to write one's own books than deal with other people's, and so I moved to the Literary Institute, where they teach you how to write.

Since then I have been writing, although, as I now realise, my true vocation is inventing. In recent years I have felt that people are beginning to impose on me the role of humorist and involuntarily somehow I am trying to live up to this imposed image.

No sooner do I make a start on something serious than I see before me the disappointed face of a reader waiting for me to have done with the official part, so to speak, and get on with something funny. This means that I have to change horses in midstream and pretend that I only started by talking seriously to make it seem all the funnier later on.

Every day, except for the days when I do something else, I shut myself up in my room, put a sheet of paper into my voracious little "Kolibri" and write, or pretend to be writing.

Usually my typewriter gives a few desultory taps and then lapses into a long silence. My family try to look as if they are creating conditions for my work and I try to look as if I am working. As a matter of fact, while sitting over my typewriter I am actually inventing something and at the same time listening for the telephone in the next room so that I can be the first to run and answer it.

The reason for this is that my daughter is also listening for the telephone to ring and, if she gets there first, she will cut off the caller with a blow of her little fist. She thinks this is a kind of game, and she is not altogether wrong.

Of all my numerous inventions I will mention here

13

only two. An instrument for stimulating spiritual activity (a kind of electromassage for the soul), and also the method of "Mother-in-Law Isolation by Shock", based entirely on Pavlov's doctrine of conditioned and unconditioned reflexes.

The instrument for stimulating spiritual activity outwardly resembles the conventional electric shaver. The difficulty of using it lies in determining the exact location of a given person's soul. Apparently the whereabouts of a man's soul in the organism depends on his character and inclinations. It may be located in the stomach, in the gall bladder, in the blind gut and, of course, in the heel. This last fact was known to the ancient Greeks. Hence the expression "heel of Achilles". The heel being the part of the body furthest removed from the brain makes communication very difficult between these two vital internal organs of the human body, that is, between the soul and the brain, and this in the course of time leads to an intellectual disease known as Chronic Mental Flatfootedness.

Regrettably, my instrument has not been widely adopted because the voltages of the systems in general use are not suitable for it.

The method of "Mother-in-Law Isolation by Shock" has, on the contrary, become perhaps a little too widespread thanks to its exceptional simplicity and practical effectiveness.

To apply this method you must, of course, have a mother-in-law and also a child. If you have both, there can be no doubt that the upbringing and particularly the feeding of the child will be in the hands of your mother-in-law. And since she will put all the overflowing energy of her love into the process, your child will quickly develop a firm dislike of food.

So, one morning when your mother-in-law seats herself formidably beside your child and starts plying him (or her) with rice pudding or something of the kind, you quietly sit down on the other side of the table and watch. From time to time, in an apparent fit of absent-mindedness you imitate the actions of your child, opening your mouth when he does and swallowing in such a way as to emphasise the futility of the whole operation.

Your child will soon begin to notice this. Though unable to grasp their full meaning, he will feel that your actions are directed against the common tyrant. He (or she) will look now at you, now at the tyrant. And if your mother-in-law keeps a stiff upper lip and pretends not to notice anything, he will call her attention to your behaviour in no uncertain manner.

Your mother-in-law then becomes nervous and starts giving you looks in which a Freudian hatred is as yet disguised under a mask of pedagogical reproach. To this you respond with a sad glance and an expression of complete submission, and also a shrug of the shoulders as if to indicate that you are not asking for anything, you are just looking, that's all. The atmosphere becomes tense.

Eventually, after the usual mythological threats or open blackmail, when the most hated spoonful of all is being thrust down the child's throat, you will say in a very quiet, uncertain voice:

"If she (or he) doesn't want it, can I finish it?"

Petrified with indignation, your mother-in-law glares at you with the expression of Tsar Peter looking at his traitor son in the famous painting by N. N. Ghe. But there is still time for her to stage a come-back, and you must be ready to prevent this.

"No, only if she doesn't want it," you say, thus explaining that there is no need for wrath. "She can eat it if she wants it."

At this point your mother-in-law faints. You pick her up quickly, and carefully — I stress the carefully because some people are rather rough — carry her to bed. Now you may calmly go about your own affairs until dinner time.

I must admit that lately I have begun to repent of discovering and popularising this method. Starkly before me rises the problem of moral responsibility for letting loose an immature idea among the masses. The indiscriminate repudiation of mothers-in-law can be attributed only to a non-historical approach to the whole problem.

15

For do not mothers-in-law in the present period of history play a most progressive role in family life?

As a matter of fact, our mother-in-law is our real wife. It is she who cooks our meals, she who looks after the house, she who brings up our children and simultaneously teaches us how to live our lives. And as if this were not enough, she gives us her own daughter to provide us with all the honey-sweet pleasures of love. Who is more noble or more self-sacrificing than she? She is surely our true wife or, at least, the senior wife in our small but close-knit harem.

Of my other minor discoveries I feel I can mention one. It concerns humour. I have a number of valuable observations on this subject. I believe that to possess a good sense of humour one must reach a state of extreme pessimism, look down into those awful depths, convince oneself that there is nothing there either, and make one's way quietly back again. Real humour is the trail we leave on the way back from the abyss.

A TIME OF LUCKY FINDS

It was a summer evening and my uncle had guests. When they ran out of wine, I was sent to the nearest shop for some more, which, as I now realise, was not altogether the best thing for my upbringing. The errand, it is true, had first been offered to my brother but he had stubbornly refused, knowing that no one in the next few hours would be likely to punish him for refusing, and that before tomorrow came he would surely get up to some trick which he would have to answer for anyway.

So off I went, running barefoot down the warm, unpaved street, bottle in one hand, money in the other. I clearly remember the quite unusual feeling of elation that came over me. It could not have been inspired by anticipation of my forthcoming purchase because in those days I showed no particular interest in such matters. Even now my interest is moderate enough.

After all, what is the beauty of wine? Only in its power to take the edge off our personal worries when we drink with friends, and fortify what we already have in common. And even if the only thing we have in common is some worry or trouble, then wine, like art, transforming grief, soothes us and gives us the strength to go on living and hoping. We experience a renewed joy in discovering one another; we feel we are all human beings and together.

To drink with any other aim in view is simply illiterate. Solitary boozing I would compare with smuggling or some kind of perversion. He who drinks alone clinks glasses with the devil.

Well, as I was saying, on my way to the shop I was seized by a strange feeling of excitement. All the time, as I ran, I kept my eyes on the ground, and now and then I seemed to see a wad of banknotes lying there. It

2—1126

would pop up in front of me and I would actually stop to make sure whether it was there or not. I realised I was imagining things but the vision was so real that I could not help stopping. Having made sure there was no money on the ground, I only became even more elatedly convinced that I was just about to find some, and on I flew.

I bounded up the wooden steps of the shop, which stood on a kind of platform, and thrust the money and the bottle into the shopkeeper's hands. While he was fetching the wine, I took one last look down, and there I actually did see a wad of paper money wrapped in a pre-war thirty-ruble note.

I picked it up, grabbed the bottle and dashed off home, half-dead with fear and joy.

"I've found some money!" I shouted, running into the room. Our guests jumped nervously, some of them even resentfully, to their feet. A hubbub arose. There turned out to be more than a hundred rubles in the packet.

"I'll go as well!" my brother cried, fired belatedly by my success.

"Get going then!" Uncle Yura, a lorry-driver, shouted. "I was the one who suggested a drink. I'm always lucky over picking things up."

"Particularly your elbow," our imperturbable Auntie Sonya put in slyly.

"Back in the old days, in Labinsk..." Uncle Pasha began. He was always telling us about his ulcer or about the wonderful life they used to lead in the Kuban country in the old days. Either he would start off about life on the Kuban and finish with his ulcer, or the other way round. But Uncle Yura shouted him down.

"It was my suggestion! I ought to get a cut!" he clamoured. Once he started there was no stopping him.

"If it was, I didn't hear it," Uncle Pasha retorted gruffly.

"You said yourself a White Cossack slashed your ear with his sabre!"

"That was my left ear and you're sitting on my right," said Uncle Pasha, delighted to have outwitted Uncle Yura, and with a well-practised movement of his huge, workman's hand folded his left ear forward. Just

18

above it there was a cleft large enough to hold a walnut. Everyone respectfully examined the scar left by the Cossack sabre.

"Yes, it seems only yesterday. We was stationed at Tikhoretsky..." Uncle Pasha resumed, trying to profit by the general attention, but Uncle Yura again interrupted him.

"If you don't believe me, let the boy say it himself." Whereupon everyone looked at me.

In those days I was fond of Uncle Yura, and of everyone else at the table. I wanted them all to enjoy my success, to feel they had all had a part in it without any advantage for anyone.

"It was everybody's suggestion," I proclaimed spiritedly.

"I'm not saying it wasn't everybody's suggestion, but who suggested it first?" Uncle Yura bawled, but his voice was drowned in a joyful burst of clapping, by which everyone sought to show that Uncle Yura was much too fond of stealing the limelight.

"Oh, Allah," said Uncle Alikhan, who was the mildest and most peaceable of men because his job was selling honey-coated almonds, "the boy has found money and they make all this noise. Wouldn't it be better to drink his health?"

This caused an even greater hubbub because all the menfolk got up and wanted to drink my health at once.

"I always knew he'd make a man..."

"May this little glass..."

"Our young people have an open road before them..."

"Here's wishing him a happy childhood..."

"And what a road it is! A first-class highway!"

"For this life," Uncle Fima was the last to proclaim, "we fought like lions, and the lion's share of us was left lying on the battlefield."

"He'll be a learned man, like you," my aunt interposed, to calm him down.

"Even more learned," Uncle Fima cried and, having elevated me to this unprecedented height, he drained his glass. Uncle Fima was the most educated man in our

19

street and therefore always the first to feel the effect of drink.

I was jubilant. I wanted to show how fond I was of everyone. I wanted to give them my word of honour that I would find for them, one and all, everything they had ever lost in life. I may not have thought in exactly those words, but that was the gist of it. However, I had no time to voice my thoughts, because mother came in and, deliberately ignoring the general merriment, plucked me out of the room like a radish out of a vegetable bed.

She didn't like my attending these festive gatherings at the best of times, added to which she was offended that I should have run past my own home with the money I had found.

"You'll be like your father, always doing your best for other people," she said as we went down the steps.

"I'll do my best for everyone," I replied.

"It doesn't work out like that," she said sadly, taken up with some thought of her own.

At that moment we met my brother returning from his search. His face showed that you can't draw the winning ticket twice over.

"Did you let them see all the money?" he asked as he went by.

"Yes," I replied proudly.

"More fool you," he snapped, and ran away.

None of these minor setbacks, however, could damp the new flame that burned within me. Already I had decided that nothing would ever go wrong or get lost in our house any more. If I could find so much money without even trying, what should I find when I was really on the look-out? The world was full of treasures, above and below ground; all you had to do was keep your eyes open and not be too lazy to pick them up.

The next morning, with the money I had found my family bought me a fine sailor's jacket with an anchor on the sleeve, which I was to wear for many years to come, and before the day was out the news of my find had spread round our yard and far beyond its borders. People dropped in to congratulate us and learn the details of this joyful event. The women eyed me with a housewife's

20

curiosity, and their glances showed that they would not have minded adopting me as their own son or, at least, borrowing me for a while.

I told the story of my discovery dozens of times, not forgetting to mention the sense of anticipation that had preceded it.

"I felt it was going to happen," I would say. "I kept looking at the ground and saw money lying there."

"Do you feel that now?"

"No, not now," I confessed honestly.

It really was a minor miracle. Now my theory is that the money had been dropped by some profiteering driver, one of the kind who often stopped at that shop for a quick drink. When he got on the road again, he must have realised his loss, and his anxious signals had been correctly decoded by my excited brain.

That very same day a woman came round from next door and congratulated my mother, then said she had lost one of her hens.

"Well, what do you expect me to do?" my mother asked severely.

"Ask your son to look for it," said the woman.

"Oh, go along, for goodness sake," mother replied. "The boy found some money for once and now we shall never have any peace."

They were talking in the corridor and I could hear them through the door. Overcome by impatience, I opened it.

"I'll find your hen," I said, peeping out cheerfully from behind mother's back. A day or two before this my ball had rolled into our neighbour's cellar. When I went to fetch it I had noticed a hen there and, since no one in our yard had complained of losing a hen, I now realised that this must be hers. "I feel it's in the cellar next door," I said after a moment's thought.

"There's no hen down there," came the unexpected retort from the owner of the cellar. She had been listening to our conversation while hanging out her washing in the yard.

"It must be," I said.

"No need to go rummaging in there, knocking down

21

the firewood. You'll only start a fire or something," she blustered.

I took a box of matches and dashed over to the cellar. The door was locked but there was a hole in the wall on the other side, through which I crawled.

It was dark inside except for a faint glimmer of light from the hole, and I had to bend down all the time.

"What's he doing in there?" came a voice from outside.

"Looking for treasure," Sonka, my scatter-brained girlfriend of those days, replied. "He's found a million."

Striking matches carefully and peering round, I reached the spot where I had seen the hen before, and there she was again. She had half risen and was craning her neck, blinking dazedly in my direction. I realised she must be sitting on some eggs. Townbred fowls usually find a hidden nook to lay their eggs. It was not difficult to catch her in the darkness. I groped in the nest she had made for herself with a few wisps of hay, and put the warm eggs into my pockets. Then I made my way back, not lighting any more matches because I was now heading for the daylight.

At the sight of the hen, its mistress started clucking with joy, just like her bird.

"That's not all," I said as I handed it over.

"What else is there?" she asked.

"Here you are," I replied, and started taking the eggs out of my pockets. For some reason the hen got annoyed at the sight of the eggs, though I had made no secret of taking them from the cellar. Perhaps she hadn't noticed what I was doing in the dark. Her mistress put the eggs in her apron and, tucking the hen under her arm, walked out of the yard.

"Come and see us when the figs are ripe," she shouted from the gate

From then on I was always on the look-out and often made some quite unexpected discoveries, with the result that I became known as a kind of domestic bloodhound. I remember a rather eccentric relative of ours who had lost his goat and wanted to take me off to his village, so that I could make a thorough search for it. I was sure of finding the goat, but mother wouldn't let me go because she was afraid I might get lost in the woods myself.

I found many other things because I was always searching and because everyone believed in my powers of detection. At home I would find chips of wood baked in with the bread, needles left sticking in cushions by our absent-minded womenfolk, old tax receipts and bonds of the new state loan.

One of our neighbours often lost her spectacles and would call me in to look for them. I soon found them, if she had not had time to sweep them out of the room with the litter. But even then I would retrieve them from the rubbish bin because they were the one thing the cats prowling round it never touched. But soon she began to lose her spectacles too often and in the end I advised her to buy a spare pair so that, having lost one pair, she could look for it with the other. She followed my advice and for a time all went well, but then she started losing the spare pair, too, so I had twice as much work to do and was compelled to keep the spare pair hidden in readiness.

I enjoyed presenting the people around me with things they had lost. I worked out my own system of search, based on the principle of first seeking the lost object in the place where it had been, and then in places where it had not been and never could have been. Much later in life I learned that this is called the dialectical unity of opposites.

If the people around me stopped losing things I sometimes had to contrive my discoveries artificially.

In the evenings I would patrol the yard like a warden and hide things that had been left lying about. Often it was some washing hanging forgotten on the line. I would toss it up into the branches of a tree and the next day, when appealed to for help, after a certain amount of thinking and asking questions about what had been hanging where, as though I were solving an equation based on the speed and direction of the wind, I would point out the lost linen to the astonished housewives and recover it from the tree myself. Of course, I was not so silly as to repeat this trick too often. Besides, there were far more real losses requiring my attention.

In all this time only one of my finds failed to please its owner. It happened like this.

There was a girl living in our yard who had recently come of age. Her name was Lyuba. Nearly all day long she would sit at the window and smile into the street, arranging her hair this way and that with a little gilded hair-comb, which I at the time mistakenly took for a gold one. At her elbow stood a gramophone with its horn turned towards the street, almost always playing one and the same tune:

Lyuba, Lyuba, Lyuba, my love...

The gramophone was like the looking-glass in Pushkin's fairy-tale; it talked all the time of its mistress. I was sure of this anyway, and so, judging by Lyuba's smiling face, was she.

One day that summer, in the rather overgrown little garden by our house I found Lyuba's comb lying in the grass. I was sure it was her comb because I had never seen another like it. The same evening I paced about the yard, waiting for sounds of panic and for someone to come out and ask me to conduct a search. But Lyuba was not to be seen and there was no sign of alarm. The next morning I was even more surprised to find no messenger at my bedside. I could only conclude that someone else must have lost the golden comb, but I had to make sure that Lyuba's was still in its place. As luck would have it, she stayed away from the window all day and appeared only in the evening. And now the gramophone was playing quite a different tune.

I didn't know what song it was but I understood that the gramophone was no longer talking about her. It was a sad song and, when Lyuba turned her back to the window, I saw that there was no comb in her hair and realised that she and the gramophone together were mourning its loss.

Her mother and father were standing at another window, leaning comfortably on the sill.

"Lyuba," I asked, when the song was over, "you haven't lost something, have you?"

"No," she said with a start of fright, and touched her hair in the very place where the comb had been before. And for some reason, she blushed so violently that I could see she knew what I was talking about. The only thing I didn't know was why she was concealing her loss.

"Didn't you lose this?" I said, and with the air of a conjurer who had grown rather tired of being gaped at by everyone I produced the golden comb from my pocket.

"Nasty little spy," she shouted quite unexpectedly and, snatching the comb away from me, ran into the room. This was a quite meaningless and foolish insult.

"Silly fool!" I shouted through the window, trying to pursue her with my voice. "You have to read books to know what a spy is."

I turned to go away but her father called me over. Now he was at the window alone. Lyuba's mother having run after her daughter into the room.

"What's this all about?" he asked, leaning out of the window.

"She lost her comb herself in the garden, and now she's cross about it," I said, and took myself off, still not realising what it was all about. That evening Lyuba got into hot water.

Later on an air force man appeared in their house, and a new record called "Dear Hometown" began to play.

A week later the air force man left and took Lyuba with him and now her mother would sit sadly at the window with the gramophone whimpering like a big faithful dog for its mistress: "Lyuba, Lyuba, my love..."

I continued my quest, venturing further and further into unexplored territory.

It was particularly rewarding to search the beach after a storm. At various times I found there a sailor's belt with a buckle, a buckle without a belt, live cartridges dating from the time of the Civil War, sea shells of all shapes and sizes, and even a dead dolphin. One day I discovered a bottle tossed up by a storm, but for some reason there was no message in it and I took it back to the shop.

Quite near town, on the bank of the River Kelasuri I found a whole creek of gold-bearing sand and spent all day standing knee-deep in the cold pale-blue water, panning for gold. I would scoop up a double handful of sand and water, then tilt my cupped hands and watch the water run away. Little golden sparks flashed in my palms, the water tickled my toes, big blobs of sunlight quivered on the crystalclear bottom of the creek, and I had never been happier in my whole life.

Later I was told that this was not gold but mica, but the feel of that cold mountain water, the hot sun, the clear bottom of the creek and the quiet happiness of the prospector is with me still. One day I made yet another discovery that I want to describe in more detail.

We used to play a game of seeing who could dive deepest. We would start at a depth of about two metres and go deeper and deeper until our breath was spent.

On the day I am speaking of another boy and I were competing in this way on the Beach of Dogs. The beach still has this name, either because it is strictly forbidden to let a dog bathe there, or because that is exactly what people do there with their dogs. Well, anyway, I made my last dive, reached the bottom, tried to scoop a handful of sand and nearly bumped my nose on a big square slab, on which I glimpsed what looked like a picture of two people.

"Ancient stone with a picture on it!" I shouted wildly as I reached the surface.

"You're kidding," the other boy said, swimming over to me and looking into my eyes.

"Word of honour!" I insisted. "It's a huge slab with prehistoric figures on it."

We began diving in turns and nearly every time we saw in the dim submarine light that white slab with its two blurred figures. Then we dived together and tried to move it, but it wouldn't budge an inch.

Eventually the cold drove us out of the water, but not before I had taken careful note of the place where we had been diving. It was exactly halfway between a buoy and an old pile sticking up out of the sea.

School began a few days later and I told our form-master about my discovery. He used to take us for geography and history. He was a powerfully built man with withered legs. A Hercules on crutches. His whole presence breathed mental vigour and spiritual integrity. In anger he was terrible. We loved him not only because he had such an interesting way of telling us about everything, but also because he treated us seriously, without that casual air of condescension in which youth always detects indifference.

"It must be an ancient Greek stela," he said, after listening attentively to my story. "That's a splendid discovery."

It was decided that we should go down to the beach after school and, if possible, lift the stone out of the water. "A stela," I kept repeating to myself with delight, and the rest of the day's lessons passed in joyful anticipation of the expedition.

So off we went down to the sea. Our P. T. instructor was sent with us as labour power. He hadn't wanted to go at first but the headmaster had managed to talk him into it. There was no one in the school that the P. T. instructor was afraid of because, as he often told us himself, he could take a job as a boxing coach any day. We believed that he could knock out the whole pedagogical council at one blow. Perhaps this was why his face always wore a somewhat contemptuous expression, which seemed to be aimed at everything that was done at school, as though he lived in expectation of the day when his one fatal blow would have to be delivered.

If anyone disobeyed him during a P. T. lesson, he could administer a mighty finger flick on the forehead, equal in impact to a jump from the sports ground wall on to the well-trodden school yard. This we all knew from experience.

We undressed and charged pell-mell into the sea. Only our form-master was left on the beach. He stood there leaning on his crutches in his immaculate white shirt with the sleeves rolled up, and waited.

There had been a storm the day before and I was afraid the water would be hazy but it was just as clear and still as before.

Reaching the spot first, I dived to the bottom and saw nothing. This didn't worry me much because I might not have got my bearings quite right. I plunged again, and again saw nothing. All round me the whole form was snorting, squealing and splashing. Most of them were simply playing about, but some must have been diving to the bottom because they brought up handfuls of sand and threw them at each other. No one reported sighting any stone. I swam over to the buoy to see whether it had come adrift, but it was still firmly anchored in its place.

Soon the P. T. instructor appeared on the scene. He had been slightly delayed by the need to put on bathing trunks.

"Well, where's the statue?" he asked, puffing as if the water was too hot for him.

"It should be here," I said, pointing.

He took a deep breath and, executing a powerful somersault, shot into the depths like a torpedo. He could certainly swim and dive, you had to give him that. He stayed under for a long time and at last came up, as if propelled by an underwater explosion.

"You've made the bottom all muddy," he said, snorting loudly, and shaking his head. "Now then, you young skeletons, off you go from here!" he bawled and, striking the water with the flat of his hand, sent a great jet of water at the other boys.

"You're not making this up, are you?" he asked me severely, still puffing and blowing as if the water was too hot for him.

"Do you think I'm crazy?" I said.

"How should I know?" he replied, surveying the surface of the water as though seeking a suitable hole to dive through. At last he found one and, having taken a deep breath, plunged again.

This time he reappeared with a chunk of rusty iron from the pile.

"Is this it?" he asked, eyes bulging from the strain.

"Do you think I'm crazy?" I said. "I saw a stone slab with people on it."

"How should I know?" he repeated and, tossing away the chunk of iron, made yet another plunge.

Left to myself, I began to think it was time to make for the beach, but anticipation of the shame I should endure in front of my form-master was stronger than fear. After all, I had seen it here. It couldn't have floated away!

This time the P. T. instructor came to the surface, spluttering with fright.

"What's happened?" I asked, frightened myself, thinking he had been stung by a sea-horse or something.

"What happened! I forgot to take a deep breath — that's what," he snorted, mimicking me wrathfully.

"So you forgot and I'm to blame," I said, offended by his tone.

The P. T. instructor was about to retort but before he could do so a girl's voice said, "What are you looking for?"

I glanced round. A strange girl was swimming cautiously towards us.

"Yesterday," the P. T. instructor began crossly, but he soon melted when he turned his head. "Well, an ancient Greek statue actually... Perhaps you'd like to dive with us?"

"I don't know how to dive," she said with a silly smile, as though inviting him to teach her. Her hair was tied up in a red scarf. The P. T. instructor gazed at this scarf in silent admiration, as if trying to puzzle out where she had got it.

"And where are you from yourself?" he asked irrelevantly, having apparently established where the headscarf had come from.

"From Moscow. Why?" the girl replied, and glanced towards the shore, striving to make up her mind whether it was dangerous to talk to strange men at such a depth.

"You're in luck," the P. T. instructor said. "I'll teach you how to dive."

This time she smiled more boldly. "No, I'd rather watch you."

"Well, if I don't come up again you can consider yourself responsible," he said, intercepting her smile with a smile of his own that he enlarged to positively brazen dimensions.

He did a particularly impressive somersault and plummeted into the depths. I realised that now he had started gallivanting he wouldn't have any more time for my stone.

"Did you really see a statue?" the girl asked and, lifting her hand out of the water, tucked a straying lock of hair under the scarf with her little finger, which in her foolishness she took to be less wet than the others.

"Not a statue but a stela," I corrected her, watching her shameless attempts to pretty herself up for the P. T. instructor.

"What is that?" she asked, calmly continuing her efforts.

I decided to take action before the P. T. instructor came up again.

"Don't interfere," I said. "Isn't the sea big enough for you? Go and swim somewhere else."

"Don't be rude, boy," she said haughtily, as though speaking to me from an upstairs window of her own house. How quick they were to sense which way the wind was blowing! She knew the P. T. instructor would appear sooner or later and take her side.

He surfaced noisily, like a dancer bursting into a ring of onlookers. He had been a very long time under water but it had been a wasted dive, because he had done it not for us but for her.

"Well, did you see it?" she asked him, as though she had been with him all along, and even swam a little closer to him.

"They're just a lot of day-dreamers!" he said, when he had got his breath back. This was his pet name for anyone he considered a weakling or good-for-nothing. "Let's have a swim instead."

"All right, but not too far", she consented, perhaps just to spite me.

"What about the stone?" I said, mournfully reminding him of duty.

"You'll get such a clump in a minute you'll be lying under that stone of yours," he explained calmly, and they swam away, his dark head with its broad sunburnt neck bobbing beside her red kerchief.

I looked at the beach. Many of the other boys were already lying on the sand, warming themselves. Our form-master was still there, leaning on his crutches, waiting for me to find the stone. Had I not seen my friend only the day before, I would have decided the whole thing had been just a dream.

I dived another ten times or so, combing the bottom all the way from the pile to the buoy. But the wretched stone had vanished. Meanwhile our form-master had called me several times but as I could not hear him very well I pretended not to have heard him at all. I felt too ashamed to come out of the water. I didn't know what I should say to him.

I was very tired, cold and had swallowed a lot of sea-water. It was becoming harder and harder to dive and I no longer went right to the bottom but merely ducked below the surface to avoid being seen. Many of the other boys had dressed by now and some had gone home, but my form-master still stood there waiting.

The P. T. instructor and the girl had gone ashore. He had carried his clothes over to her place and they were sitting together, talking and throwing pebbles into the sea.

I was hoping they would all go away soon and let me get out of the water. But my form-master was still there, so I went on diving.

The P. T. instructor had now tied the girl's scarf round his own head. While I was wondering why he had done this, he suddenly did a hand-stand and she started timing him with his watch. He stood on his hands for a long time and actually talked to her in this position, which she, of course, found very amusing.

I admired him mournfully for a moment, and just then my form-master shouted to me very loudly and startled me into looking at him. Our eyes met and now there was nothing I could do but swim ashore.

"You must be frozen," he shouted, when I swam nearer.

"You don't believe me, do you?" I said through chattering teeth, and crawled out of the water.

"Why shouldn't I believe you?" he said severely, leaning forward and gripping his crutches tightly with his gladiator's hands. "But you've been bathing far too long. Lie down at once!"

"There was a boy with me," I said in the whining voice of the failure. "I'll point him out to you tomorrow."

31

"Lie down!" he commanded and took a step towards me. But I stood my ground because I felt it would be hard enough for me to argue with them standing, let alone lying down.

"Perhaps that boy has pulled it out already?" one of our lads asked. That was a tempting suggestion. I looked at my form-master and realised from his glance that he was expecting only the truth, and that what I was going to say would be the truth, and so I just couldn't lie. I was too proud of the trust he had placed in me.

"No," I said, regretting, as always in such cases, that I was not lying, "I saw him yesterday and he would have told me."

"Perhaps a fish found it and carried it away," the same lad added, hopping about with his head on one side to get the water out of his ear.

That was the first jibe and I knew there were more to come, but our form-master put a stop to all that with a glance, and said, "If I didn't believe you I should never have come here in the first place." He looked thoughtfully at the sea and added, "It must have been dragged down into the sand or carried away by the storm."

But fifteen years later the stela was found, not very far from the spot where I had seen it. And the person who found it, incidentally, was my friend's brother. So I was in on that too.

The experts say it is a rare and valuable work of art — a stela with a gentle and sorrowful bas-relief that had once marked a grave.

I remember our form-master with affection and pride, his thick curly hair and fine aquiline features, the face of a Greek god, a god with crippled legs.

Our seas have no tides, but the land of childhood is like a beach, wet and mysterious after the tide has gone out, where one may find the most unexpected things.

I was always out there searching and perhaps it made me a little absent-minded. Later on, when I grew up, that is, when I had something to lose, I realised that all the lucky finds of childhood are the secret loans granted to us by fate, which afterwards, as adults, we must redeem. And justly so.

And another thing I came to understand was that everything that is lost may be found — even love, even youth. The one thing that can never be found again is a lost conscience.

But even that is not so sad a thought as it may appear if one remembers that it cannot be lost simply through absent-mindedness.

THE COCK

As a boy I was much disliked by all farmyard cocks. I don't remember what started it, but if a warlike cock appeared in the neighbourhood there was bound to be bloodshed.

One summer I was staying with my relatives in one of the mountain villages of Abkhazia. The whole family — the mother, two grown-up daughters, two grown-up sons — went off to work early in the morning to weed maize or pick tobacco. I was left behind in the house alone. My duties were pleasant and easy to perform. I had to feed the goats (one good bundle of rustling hazel-nut branches), draw fresh water from the stream for the midday break and in general keep an eye on the house. There was nothing special to keep an eye on, but now and then I had to give a shout to make the hawks feel there was a man in the vicinity and refrain from attacking our chickens. In return for this I, as a representative of the feeble urban branch of the family, was allowed to suck a pair of fresh eggs straight from the nest, which I did both gladly and conscientiously.

Fixed along the outside wall of the kitchen there were some baskets in which the hens laid their eggs. How they knew they were supposed to lay them there was always a mystery to me. I would stand on tip-toe and grope about until I found an egg. Feeling simultaneously like a successful pearl diver and the thief of Baghdad, I would break the top by tapping it on the wall and suck the egg dry at once. Somewhere nearby the hens would be clucking mournfully. Life seemed significant and full of wonder. The air was healthy, the food was healthy, and I swelled with juice like a pumpkin on a well-manured allotment.

In the house I found two books: Mayne Reid's *The*

Headless Horseman and *The Tragedies and Comedies* of William Shakespeare. The first book swept me off my feet. The very names of the characters were music to my ears: Maurice the Mustanger, Louise Pointdexter, Captain Cassius Calhoun, El Coyote, and the magnificent Dona Isidora Covarubio de los Llanos.

"'My pistol is at your head! I have one shot left — an apology, or you die!'...

"'It's the mirage!' the Captain exclaimed with the addition of an oath to give vent to his chagrin."

I read that book from beginning to end, then from the end to the beginning, and skipped through it twice.

Shakespeare's tragedies seemed to me muddled and pointless. On the other hand, the comedies fully justified the author's efforts at composition. I realised that it was not the jesters who depended on the royal courts but the royal courts that depended on the jesters.

The house we lived in stood on a hill and the winds blew round it and through it twenty-four hours a day. It was as dry and sturdy as a veteran mountaineer.

The eaves of the small veranda were tufted with swallows' nests. The swallows dived swiftly and accurately into the veranda and hovered with fluttering wings at a nest, where their greedy, vociferous young waited open-beaked, almost falling out in their eagerness. Their gluttony was matched only by the tireless energy of their parents. Sometimes having fed its young, the father would hang for a few moments leaning back from the edge of the nest, its arrow-shaped body motionless and only the head turning warily this way and that. One more instant and it would drop like a stone, then deftly level out and soar away from the veranda.

The chickens foraged peacefully in the yard, the sparrows and chicks twittered. But the demons of rebellion were not slumbering. Despite my preventive shouts, a hawk came over nearly every day. In a diving or low-level attack, it would snatch up a chicken and with mighty sweeps of its burdened wings make off in the direction of the forest. It was a breath-taking sight and I would sometimes let it get away on purpose and shout later just to soothe my conscience. The captured chicken hung in an attitude of terror and foolish submission. If I made enough noise in time, the hawk would either miss its prey or drop it in flight. In such cases we would find the chicken somewhere in the bushes, glassy-eyed and paralysed with fright.

"She's a goner," one of my cousins would say, cheerfully chopping off its head and marching away to the kitchen with the carcass.

The chief of this barnyard kingdom was a huge, red-feathered cock, rich in plumage and cunning as an oriental despot. Within a few days of my arrival it became obvious that he hated me and was only looking for a pretext to come openly to blows. Perhaps he had noticed that I was eating a lot of eggs and this offended his male vanity? Or was he infuriated by my half-heartedness during the hawk attacks? I think both these things had their effect on him but his chief grudge was that someone was challenging his power over the hens. Like any other despot, this he would not tolerate.

I realised that dual power could not last long and, in preparation for the forthcoming battle, kept him under close observation.

No one could deny the cock his share of personal bravery. During the hawk attacks, when the hens and chickens would flutter clucking and squawking in all directions, he alone would remain in the yard and, gobbling fiercely, try to restore order in his timid harem. He would even take a few resolute steps in the direction of the swooping foe, but since nothing that runs can overtake that which flies, this made an impression of mere bravado.

Usually he would forage in the yard or the kitchen garden accompanied by two or three of his favourite hens but without losing sight of the others. Now and then he would crane his neck and look up at the sky in search of danger,

As soon as the shadow of a gliding hawk passed over the yard or the cawing of a crow was heard, he would throw up his head belligerently and signal his charges to be on the alert. The hens would listen in a scared fashion and sometimes scuttle away for cover. More often than not it was a false alarm, but by keeping his numerous mistresses in a state of nervous tension he crushed their will and achieved complete submission.

As he scratched the ground with his horny claws he would sometimes discover a delicate morsel and summon the hens with loud cries to join in the feast.

While the hen that got there first was pecking his find, he would circle round her a few times, dragging his wing exuberantly and apparently choking with delight. This operation usually ended in rape. The hen would shake herself bemusedly, trying to recover her senses and grasp what had happened, while he looked round in victorious satisfaction.

If the wrong hen ran up in response to his call, he would guard his find or drive her away while continuing to summon his new beloved with loud grunting noises. His favourite was a neat white hen, as slim as a pullet. She would approach him cautiously, stretch out her neck, cleverly scoop up the morsel and run away as hard as she could, showing no signs of gratitude whatever.

He would pound after her humiliatedly, trying to keep up appearances though well aware of the indignity of his position. Usually he failed to catch her and would eventually come to a halt, breathing heavily and trying to look at me as though nothing had happened and his little trot had been entirely for his own pleasure.

Actually the invitations to a feast were quite often sheer deception. He had nothing worth eating and the hens knew it, but they were betrayed by their eternal feminine curiosity.

As the days went by he grew more and more insolent. If I happened to be crossing the yard he would run after me for a short distance just to test my courage. Despite the shivers going down my spine I would nevertheless stop and wait to see what would follow. He would stop, too, and wait. But the storm was bound to break and break it did.

One day, when I was eating in the kitchen, he marched in and planted himself in the doorway. I threw him a few pieces of hominy but to no avail. He pecked up my offering but I could see he had no intention of making peace.

There was nothing for it. I brandished a halfburnt log at him but he merely gave a little jump, stuck out his neck like a gander and stared at me with hate-filled eyes. Then I threw the log. It fell beside him. He jumped even higher and flung himself at me, belching a stream of barnyard abuse. A flaming red ball of hate came flying towards me. I managed to shield myself with a stool. He flew straight into it and collapsed on the floor like a slain dragon. While he was getting up, his wings beat on the earthen floor, raising spurts of dust and chilling my legs with the wind of battle.

I managed to change my position and retreat towards the door, protecting myself with the stool like a Roman legionary with his shield.

As I was crossing the yard he charged several times. Whenever he came at me I felt as if he was going to peck my eyes out. I made good use of the stool and he bounced off it regularly on to the ground. My hands were scratched and bleeding and the heavy stool was becoming ever harder to hold. But it was my only means of protection.

One more attack. With a mighty sweep of his wings the cock flew up and, instead of colliding with my shield, unexpectedly perched on top of it.

I threw the stool down and in a few bounds reached the veranda, and from there darted into the room slamming the door benind me.

My chest was humming like a telegraph pole and my hands were streaming with blood. I stood and listened. I was sure that the wretched cock was lurking at the door. And so he was. After a while he moved away a little and began to march up and down the veranda, his iron claws clacking loudly on the floor. He was calling me out to do battle but I preferred to lie low in my stronghold. At length he grew tired of waiting and, perched on the railing, gave vent to a victorious cock-a-doodle-doo.

When my cousins learnt of my affray with the cock, they started holding daily tournaments. Neither of us gained any decisive advantage and we all went about with scratches and bruises.

The fleshy, tomato-like comb of my opponent bore several marks of the stick and his glorious fountain of a tail showed signs of drying up, but from losing any of his self-assurance he had become all the more insolent. He had acquired an annoying habit of crowing from a perch on the rail of the veranda, just under the window of the room where I slept. Evidently he regarded the veranda as occupied territory.

Our battles were held in all kinds of places, in the yard, in the kitchen garden, in the orchard. If I climbed a tree for figs or for apples, he would stand and wait for me patiently beneath.

To cure him of some of his arrogance I resorted to various stratagems. I started treating the hens to extra food. He would fly into a rage when I called them but they treacherously deserted him all the same. Persuasion was useless. Here, as in any other field, abstract propaganda was easily deflated by the reality of profit. The handfuls of maize that I tossed out of the window conquered the tribal loyalty and family traditions of the valorous egg-layers. In the end the pasha himself would appear. He would reproach them indignantly but they, merely pretending to be ashamed of their weakness, went on pecking up the maize.

One day, when my aunt and her sons were working in the kitchen garden, we had another encounter. By this time I was an experienced and cold-blooded warrior. I found a forked stick and, using it like a trident, after a few unsuccessful attempts pinned the cock to the ground. His powerful body writhed frantically and its vibrations came up the stick like an electric current.

I was inspired by the madness of the brave. Without letting go of the stick or releasing its pressure, I bent down and, seizing my chance, pounced on the cock like a goalkeeper on a ball and managed to seize him by the throat. He writhed vigorously and dealt me such a blow on the head with his wing that I went deaf in one ear. Fear reinforced my courage. I squeezed his throat even tighter. Hard and sinewy, it jerked and twisted in my hand and I felt as if I were holding a snake. With the other hand I grasped his legs. His long claws worked desperately to reach my body and fasten on to some part of it.

But the trick was done. I straightened up and the cock hung suspended by his feet, emitting stifled squawks.

All this time my cousins and aunt had been roaring with laughter as they watched us from behind the fence. So much the better! Great waves of joy flowed through me. In a very short time, however, I felt rather confused. My vanquished opponent showed no signs of giving in. He was throbbing with a furious desire for revenge. If I let him go, he would come at me again, and yet I couldn't go on holding him like this forever.

"Throw him over the fence," my aunt advised.

I went up to the fence and tossed him over with leaden arms.

Curse it all! He, of course, did not fly over the fence but perched on it, spreading his massive wings. The next moment he flung himself at me. This was too much. I made a wild dash for safety and from my breast rose the ancient cry for help of all fleeing children:

"Mummy!"

One must be very foolish or very brave to turn one's back on an enemy. In my case it was certainly not bravery, and I paid the price for it.

He caught me several times while I was running till at last I tripped and fell. He sprang on top of me, he rolled on me, he gurgled with bloodthirsty glee. He might quite easily have pecked through my spine if my cousin had not run up and knocked him off into the bushes with his hoe. We decided that this had killed him, but in the evening the cock came out of the bushes, subdued and saddened.

As she bathed my wounds, my aunt said, "It doesn't look as if you two will ever get on together. We'll roast him tomorrow."

The next day my cousin and I set about catching the cock. The poor fellow sensed that fate had turned against him. He fled from us with the speed of an ostrich. He flew into the kitchen garden, he hid in the bushes. Finally he flapped into the cellar, and there we caught him. He looked persecuted and his eyes were full of mournful reproach He seemed to be saying to me, "Yes, we were foes, you and I. But it was an honourable war, between men. I never expected such treachery from you." I felt strangely upset and turned away. A few minutes later my cousin lopped off his head. The cock's body jerked and writhed, the wings flapped and folded as if to cover the gushing throat. Life would be safer now but all the fun had gone out of it.

Still, he made us a fine dinner, and the spicy nut sauce that went with it diluted the pangs of my unexpected sorrow.

Now I realise that he was really a splendid fighting cock, but born too late. The days of cock fighting have long since passed, and fighting the human race is a lost cause from the start.

THE THIRTEENTH LABOUR
OF HERCULES

Nearly all the mathematicians I have ever known have been untidy, slack and rather brilliant individuals. So the saying about the perfection of Pythagoras's pants is probably not absolutely correct.

Pythagoras's pants may have been perfect but his disciples seem to have forgotten the fact and pay little attention to their own appearance.

Yet, there was one teacher of mathematics at our school who differed from all others. He was neither slack nor untidy. I don't know whether he was brilliant or not, and that is now rather difficult to establish. I think he probably was.

His name was Kharlampy Diogenovich. So, like Pythagoras, he was of Greek origin. He appeared in our form at the beginning of a school year. We had never heard of him before and had never suspected that such mathematicians could exist.

He immediately established the rule of exemplary silence in our form. The silence was so terrifying that our headmaster would sometimes throw open the form-room door in alarm because he was not sure whether we were at our desks or had all run away to the sports ground.

The sports ground bordered on the school yard and at all times, particularly during important competitions, interfered with the pedagogical process. Our headmaster had actually written a letter requesting that it should be moved elsewhere. He maintained that the sports ground upset his pupils. In fact, we were upset not by the sports ground but by the groundsman, Uncle Vasya, who never failed to recognise us, even without our books, and chased us out of his domain with a wrathful zeal that showed no sign of waning with the years.

Luckily, no one listened to our headmaster and the sports ground stayed where it was, except that the wooden fence was replaced by a brick wall. So even those who used to watch events through the chinks in the fence now had to climb the wall.

Nevertheless, our headmaster had no reason to be afraid of our absenting ourselves from a mathematics lesson. This was unthinkable. It would have been just as bad as going up to the headmaster between lessons and silently snatching off his hat, although everyone was utterly fed up with that hat. He went about in it all the year round, winter and summer, always the same soft felt hat, evergreen like a magnolia. And was always afraid of something.

To the uninitiated it might have appeared that what he feared most was the commission of the City Department of Public Education, but in fact there was no one he feared more than our director of studies, a demon of a woman about whom I shall one day write a poem in Byronic vein. At the moment, however, I have a different story to tell.

Of course, we could never have escaped from a mathematics lesson. If we ever managed to miss a lesson, it was usually singing.

As soon as our Kharlampy Diogenovich entered the room, the whole form would fall silent and remain so till the end of the lesson. True, he sometimes made us laugh, but this was not spontaneous laughter; it was amusement master-minded from above by the teacher himself. Far from destroying discipline, it actually ministered to it, just as a converse proposition assists proof in geometry.

This is how it worked. Let us suppose that a pupil was late for a lesson and arrived, say, about half a second after the bell had rung, when Kharlampy Diogenovich would be on the point of entering the room himself. The wretched pupil would be wishing he could fall through the floor, and would have done so if the teachers' common room had not been underneath.

Some teachers paid no attention to such a minor offence, others would flare up and give you a reprimand on the spot; but not Kharlampy Diogenovich. In such cases he would halt in the doorway, shift his register from one hand to the other and with a gesture full of respect for his pupil motion him towards the door.

The pupil would hesitate and his embarrassed face would express a fervent desire to somehow creep in behind his teacher. Kharlampy Diogenovich's face, on the other hand, would effuse a joyous hospitality moderated only by politeness and an understanding of the peculiar demands of the situation. He would make it felt that the mere arrival of such a pupil was a delightful occasion for the whole form and himself personally, that none of us had been expecting him but now that he was here no one would dare to reproach him for being a mere fraction of a second late, least of all he, a humble schoolmaster, who would naturally enter the form-room behind such a splendid pupil and himself close the door after him to show that we were not going to let our dear guest out again in a hurry.

The whole thing would last only a few seconds, at the end of which the pupil, having edged awkwardly through the door, would stumble on towards his desk.

Kharlampy Diogenovich would watch his progress and make some splendid comment. For example, "The Prince of Wales."

The form would roar with laughter. Though we had no idea who the Prince of Wales was, we realised that he could not possibly appear in our form. For one thing there would be no point in it because princes were mainly engaged in chasing the deer. And if this particular prince had got tired of chasing his deer and felt like visiting a school, they would be sure to take him to School No. l, near the power station, because it was a model school. At any rate, if he had insisted on coming to ours, we should have been warned long beforehand and thoroughly briefed for his arrival.

This was why we laughed, realising that our pupil could not possibly be a prince, and certainly not any Prince of Wales.

But the moment Kharlampy Diogenovich sat down at his desk the form would fall silent and the lesson would begin.

A shortish man with a large head, neatly dressed and carefully shaved, he controlled his form with calm authority. Besides the form register he kept a notebook in which he made notes after testing a boy's knowledge. I cannot remember him ever raising his voice at anyone or urging him to work harder or threatening to send for his parents. He had no use for such methods.

During a test he never stalked about between the desks, peering inside or looking round vigilantly at the slightest rustle as other teachers did. Nothing of the kind. He would sit at his own desk, reading calmly or fingering a string of yellow beads, which looked like cat's eyes.

Cribbing during his lessons was almost useless because he never failed to recognise something that had been copied, and would hold it up to ridicule. So we cribbed only in cases of extreme emergency, when there was no other way out.

Sometimes during a test he would relinquish his beads or book for a moment and say:

"Sakharov, would you mind going and sitting next to Avdeyenko, please."

Sakharov would stand up and stare questioningly at Kharlampy Diogenovich, unable to understand why he, one of the best boys in the form, should be relegated to a place next to Avdeyenko, who was an absolute dud.

"Take pity on Avdeyenko. I'm afraid he will break his neck."

Avdeyenko would gaze stolidly at Kharlampy Diogenovich as though — or perhaps because — he could not understand why he was in danger of breaking his neck.

"Avdeyenko thinks he is a swan," Kharlampy Diogenovich would explain. "A black swan," he would add a moment later, alluding perhaps to Avdeyenko's sullen sunburnt face. "Carry on, Sakharov."

Sakharov would sit down again.

"You may carry on too," Kharlampy Diogenovich would tell Avdeyenko, but with a perceptible change of voice, which now carried a carefully measured dose of sarcasm. "If you don't break your neck of course, Black Swan!" he would conclude firmly, his final phrase somehow expressing the valiant hope that Avdeyenko would acquire the ability to work on his own.

Shurik Avdeyenko would pore furiously over his exercise book, demonstrating a great effort of mind and will directed to this end.

Kharlampy Diogenovich's chief weapon was his knack of ridicule. The pupil who defied the school rules was not a slacker, not a dud, not a hooligan, he was simply funny. Or rather, not simply funny — many of us would not have minded that at all — but ridiculous. Ridiculous without realising that he was ridiculous, or being the last to guess it.

When a teacher makes you appear ridiculous, you immediately lose the traditional support of the rest of the form and they all laugh at you. It is all against one. If one person laughs at you, you can usually deal with the situation somehow. But you cannot turn the laugh against the whole form. Once in this ridiculous position, you will go to any lengths to prove yourself a little less ridiculous than you inevitably appear.

Kharlampy Diogenovich had no favourites. We were all potential victims of his wit and I, of course, was no exception.

That day I had not solved the problem we had been set for homework. It had been about an artillery shell flying somewhere at a certain speed for a certain time. We had to work out how many kilometres it would have flown if it had been travelling at a different speed and, perhaps, even in a different direction.

As if one and the same shell could possibly fly at different speeds. It was a muddled, stupid kind of problem and my answer just wouldn't come out right. Incidentally, the answers given at the back of some of the textbooks in those years — it must have been sabotage — were incorrect. This did not happen very often, of course, because by that time nearly all the saboteurs had been caught. But apparently there were one or two still at large.

However, I was still troubled with doubts. Saboteurs may be saboteurs, but it's no good relying on them.

So, the next day I arrived at school a whole hour before lessons started. We were in the second shift. The keenest footballers were in the yard already. I asked one of them about the problem and it turned out that he had not been able to get it right either. That set my conscience completely at rest. We split up into two teams and played till the bell rang for school.

In we went. Almost before I had got my breath back, I asked our top boy Sakharov,

"Well, how about that problem?"

"Not so bad," he said. "I solved it."

He gave a brief, meaningful nod, indicating that there had been certain difficulties but he had surmounted them.

"How could you? The answer in the back is wrong."

"No, it isn't," he said, nodding again, this time with such an annoying expression of assurance on his clever, conscientious face that I at once began to hate him for his good fortune. I was about to express a few more doubts but he turned away, thus depriving me of the falling man's last consolation — grabbing at air.

Apparently, at that moment Kharlampy Diogenovich had appeared in the doorway but I had failed to notice him and continued my gesticulations, although he was only a few feet away from me. At length I realised what had happened, closed my textbook in frightened haste and froze to my desk.

Kharlampy Diogenovich took his place by the blackboard.

I cursed myself for at first agreeing with the footballer that the solution in the book was wrong, and afterwards agreeing with the top boy that it was right. Now Kharlampy Diogenovich would be sure to notice my anxiety and call me to the board first.

Next to me sat a quiet and meek member of the form, whose name was Adolf Komarov. Nowadays he called himself Alik Komarov and even wrote Alik on his copybooks because the war had started and he did not want to be nicknamed Hitler. It made no difference. Everyone remembered his proper name and reminded him of it whenever they had the chance.

I liked talking in class and he liked keeping quiet. We had been put together to exert a good influence on each other but it hadn't worked. Neither of us had changed.

Now I noticed that even he had solved the problem. He was sitting over his open notebook, neat, thin and quiet, and his hands lying on the blotting paper before him made him seem even quieter. He had this stupid habit of keeping his hands on his blotter, of which I just could not break him.

"Hitler *kaput*," I whispered in his direction. He made no reply, of course, but at least he took his hands off his blotter, which was some relief.

Meanwhile Kharlampy Diogenovich greeted the form and sat down in his chair. He flicked back the sleeves of his jacket, slowly wiped his nose and mouth with a handkerchief, which he examined for some reason, then put away in his pocket. After that he removed his watch and began to thumb through the pages of the register. It looked as if the executioner was speeding up his preparations.

At last, however, he finished marking those absent and looked round the room, selecting his victim. I held my breath.

"Who's the monitor?" he asked unexpectedly. I sighed with relief, thanking him for the respite.

There turned out to be no monitor for that day and Kharlampy Diogenovich told our form captain to wipe the board. While he was doing so, Kharlampy Diogenovich lectured him on the duties of a form captain when there was no monitor. I began to hope he would tell us some story connected with the subject, or one of Aesop's fables, or something out of Greek mythology. But he refrained from any further illustration of his lecture because the scrape of the dry rag on the blackboard was distracting and he was anxious for the form captain to finish his irritating task. At last the form captain returned to his place.

We waited in suspense. But at that moment the door opened and a woman doctor and a nurse appeared.

"Excuse me, is this 5A?" the doctor asked.

"No, it is not," Kharlampy Diogenovich replied with polite hostility, seeing that some medical project was about to interfere with his lesson. Although our form was nearly 5A, because it was 5B, he had answered as firmly as if we had absolutely nothing in common. "Excuse me," the doctor said again and, after lingering for a moment, withdrew and closed the door.

I knew they were going to innoculate us against typhus.

48

Some of the forms had been done already. Innoculations were never announced beforehand so that no one could slip away or stay at home on the pretext of being ill.

I was not afraid of innoculations because I had had plenty, against malaria, the nastiest of all.

And now the white-coated hope that had suddenly illuminated our form had disappeared. I just could not let that happen.

"May I show them where 5A is?" I said, growing quite brazen in my fear.

There were two factors to justify the audacity of my proposal. My place was near the door and I was often sent to the teachers' room for chalk and other things of that kind. Besides, form 5A was situated in an annexe in the school yard and the doctor might indeed get lost because she was permanently attached to School No. 1 and rarely visited us.

"Yes, do," Kharlampy Diogenovich said, and raised his eyebrows slightly.

Trying to conceal my joy, I shot out of the room.

I caught up the doctor and nurse while they were still in the corridor on our floor.

"I'll show you where 5A is," I said, falling into step beside them.

The doctor smiled as if she was handing out sweets instead of innoculations.

"Aren't you going to do us?" I asked.

"During the next lesson," the doctor said, still smiling.

"But we are going out to the museum for the next lesson," I said, rather to my own surprise.

There had, in fact, been some talk of our making an organised visit to the local museum to see the prehistoric remains on show there. But our history mistress kept putting it off because the headmaster was afraid we might not get there in an organised fashion.

Last year a boy in our form had stolen a dagger that had once belonged to an Abkhazian feudal prince, because he wanted to run away to the front with it. This had caused a great rumpus and the headmaster had decided that it had all come about because the form had wandered

49

down to the museum in a crowd instead of marching there in double file.

In fact, that lad had worked everything out very carefully long beforehand. Instead of taking the dagger at once, he had hidden it in the thatch of an exhibit labelled Prerevolutionary Poor Man's Hovel, and only months later, when the fuss had died down, did he go there in a coat with a slit in the lining and complete his theft.

"We won't let you," the doctor said cheerfully.

"But we're all going to assemble in the yard," I said, getting worried, "and go on an organised visit to the museum."

"So it's an organised visit, is it?"

"Yes, it is," I said seriously, afraid that she, too, like our headmaster, would doubt our ability to visit the museum in an organised fashion.

"Well, Galochka, let's go back to 5B, just in case," the doctor said, and stopped. I had always liked these nice clean women doctors in their little white caps and white coats.

"But they told us to go to 5A first," that stubborn creature Galochka protested, and looked at me severely. Anyone could see she was trying to make herself out a grown-up.

I never gave her so much as a glance, just to show that nobody would ever take her for one.

"What difference does it make," the doctor said, and clinched the argument by turning round.

"So you can't wait to show us how brave you are?" she added.

"I'm a malaria sufferer," I said, dismissing the implication of self-interest. "I've had thousands of injections."

"Well, lead on then, malaria sufferer," said the doctor, and we started back.

Having made sure they were not going to change their minds, I ran on ahead so as to cut out any connection between myself and their arrival.

When I entered the form-room, Shurik Avdeyenko was at the blackboard and, although the solution to the problem was written out in three stages on the blackboard in his beautiful handwriting, he could not explain it. He stood there with an expression of sullen fury on his face, as though he had known just how it went before but was now unable to recall the course of his reasoning.

Don't worry, Shurik, I thought. You may not know it but I've saved you already. Now I wanted to be kind and benevolent to everyone.

"Good work, Alik," I said as I took my place beside Komarov. "Fancy solving such a difficult problem."

Alik was considered a good plodder. He was rarely reprimanded and even more rarely praised. Now the tips of his ears blushed gratefully. He bent over his exercise book once more and placed his hands neatly on the blotter. Oh well, I suppose he just couldn't help it.

A few moments later the door opened and the doctor and that Galochka kid entered the room. The doctor said the whole form had to be innoculated.

"If it must be done now," said Kharlampy Diogenovich, with a quick glance in my direction, "how can I object? Go back to your place, Avdeyenko," he added with a nod at Shurik.

Shurik put down the chalk and walked back to his desk, still pretending to be engaged in a concentrated effort of recall.

A stir of excitement passed through the form but Kharlampy Diogenovich raised his eyebrows and all was calm. He put his notepad away in his pocket, closed the register, relinquished his place to the doctor and himself sat down at one of the desks, looking sad and rather hurt.

The doctor and the girl opened their bags and started setting out on the table bottles, jars and wickedly gleaming instruments.

"Well, who's the bravest boy in the form?" the doctor said, sucking serum greedily into the syringe and holding it point upwards to prevent any dripping out.

She spoke cheerfully but no one smiled. All eyes were on the needle.

"We'll have to call them out in alphabetical order," said Kharlampy Diogenovich. "Everyone is a hero in this form."

He opened the register.

51

"Avdeyenko," he said, looking up.

The form laughed nervously, and even the doctor smiled, although she had no idea what we were laughing at.

Avdeyenko went to the table, a tall, ungainly figure whose face clearly revealed that he had not yet made up his mind whether it was better to get a bad mark or be the first for innoculation.

He pulled up his shirt and stood with his back to the doctor, looking even more ungainly and still uncertain which was better. When it was all over and he had been innoculated, he looked just as unhappy, although he was now envied by the whole form.

Alik Komarov grew more and more pale as his turn approached and, although he kept his hands on the blotting paper in front of him, I could see it was not helping at all.

I tried to cheer him up but it was no good. He grew paler and sterner every minute, his eyes fixed unwaveringly on the doctor's needle.

"Turn your head away," I told him.

"I can't," he replied in an agonised whisper.

"It won't hurt much at first," I encouraged him. "The time it hurts most is when the serum starts going in."

"I'm so thin," he whispered back, scarcely moving his white lips. "It'll hurt me terribly."

"Don't worry," I said. "You'll be all right as long as it doesn't touch the bone."

"I'm nothing but bones," he whispered desperately. "It's sure to touch one."

"Relax your muscles," I said, patting him on the shoulder. "Nothing will touch the bone then."

"I haven't got any muscles," he replied dully, "and I'm anaemic."

"Thin people are never anaemic," I retorted strictly "Malaria sufferers are anaemic because malaria sucks their blood",

I suffered from chronic malaria and the doctors could do nothing about it however much they treated me. I was rather proud of my incurable malaria.

By the time they called Alik's name, he was in a real state. He hardly knew where he was going or what for.

He stood with his back to the doctor, white-faced

and glassy-eyed and when she made the injection he suddenly went pale as death, although it had seemed impossible for him to get any paler. He turned so pale that his face came out in freckles. None of us had thought he was freckled before and I decided to keep the fact of his concealed freckles in mind. It might come in useful one day, although I had no idea what for.

After the injection he nearly collapsed but the doctor held him up and helped him to a chair. His eyes rolled back alarmingly and we thought he was going to die.

"Ambulance!" I shouted. "I'll go and call the ambulance!"

Kharlampy Diogenovich looked at me wrathfully and the doctor deftly put a bottle of smelling salts under his nose — not Kharlampy Diogenovich's, of course, but Alik's.

At first he wouldn't open his eyes, then he suddenly jumped to his feet and marched smartly back to his place, as though it certainly was not Alik Komarov who had been just about to die.

"Didn't feel a thing," I said, when I had my injection, though I had felt it quite distinctly.

"Well done, malaria sufferer," said the doctor.

Her assistant dabbed my back carelessly after the injection. I could see she was still annoyed with me for not letting them go to 5A.

"Rub harder," I said. "The serum must be made to circulate."

She finished rubbing my back with an energy born of hatred. It was pleasant to feel the cool cotton wool soaked in surgical spirit, and even more pleasant to know that, even though she was angry with me, she still had to rub my back.

At last the whole thing was over. The doctor and her Galochka packed their bags and went on their way, leaving a pleasant smell of surgical spirit and an unpleasant smell of serum in the room. The pupils sat at their desks, fidgeting and cautiously feeling for the effects of the injection with their shoulder blades and talking freely to each other as a reward for the suffering they had just endured.

"Open the window," said Kharlampy Diogenovich, resuming his seat. He wanted this spirit of hospital freedom to depart along with the smell of medicine.

He took out his yellow beads and flicked them thoughtfully to and fro. There was not much of the lesson left. He usually filled in such gaps by telling us something instructive connected with the ancient Greeks.

"As we know from Greek mythology, Hercules had to perform twelve labours," he said, and stopped. *Click-click* — as two beads slid from right to left. "But a certain young man thought he would revise Greek mythology," he added, and stopped again. *Click-click*.

That fellow had too big an idea of himself, I thought, realising that no one was allowed to revise Greek mythology. Some other God-forsaken mythology, perhaps, might be knocked into shape but not Greek mythology because it had all been revised from beginning to end already and there couldn't possibly be any mistakes in it.

"He decided to perform the thirteenth labour of Hercules," Kharlampy Diogenovich went on. "And to some extent he succeeded."

We realised at once by his voice what a false and futile labour this had been, because if there had been any need for Hercules to perform thirteen labours he would have performed them himself, but since he had stopped at twelve it meant that twelve were enough and there was no need for anyone to mess about making corrections.

"Hercules performed his labours like a hero. But this young man performed his labour out of cowardice." Kharlampy Diogenovich paused thoughtfully, then added, "In a moment we shall learn just what it was that induced him to perform this labour."

Click. This time only one bead slid from right to left, driven by a very sharp flip of the finger. It slid rather nastily somehow. Two beads sliding together, as they had done before, would have been better than just one, all by itself.

I caught the scent of danger in the air. It was the sound not of a bead sliding but of a small trap closing in Kharlampy Diogenovich's hands.

"I have a feeling that I know already what it was," he said, and looked at me.

54

Something in his glance made my heart thud heavily against my spine.

"Be so kind," he said, and beckoned me to the blackboard.

"Who? Me?" I asked, feeling as if my voice was coming from the pit of my stomach.

"Yes, you, my fearless malaria sufferer," he said.

I shambled towards the board.

"Tell us how you solved the problem," he said calmly and — *click, click* — two more beads went sliding from right to left. I was in his hands.

The form looked on and waited. They were all expecting me to come to grief, and they wanted me to do so as slowly and interestingly as possible.

I squinted at the board from the corner of my eye, trying to trace the thread of cause and effect between the stages of the problem that were written there, but it was no use. Then with a great show of impatience I began rubbing it all out, as though what Shurik had written was muddling me and preventing me from concentrating. I was still hoping for the bell to ring and save me from execution. But the bell did not ring and it was impossible to go on cleaning the board forever. I put down the rag to avoid looking ridiculous before I had to.

"We are listening," Kharlampy Diogenovich said, without looking at me.

"An artillery shell..." I said brightly amid the form's jubilant silence, and broke off.

"Continue," Kharlampy Diogenovich said, after waiting politely for some moments.

"An artillery shell..." I repeated stubbornly, hoping that the impetus of these correct words would carry me on to more, similarly correct words. But something held me on a firm tether that pulled tight as soon as the words were out of my mouth.

I concentrated fiercely, trying to imagine the course of the problem, and then plunged forward again to break the invisible tether.

"An artillery shell..." I repeated, quivering with horror and revulsion.

A few restrained titters came from the form. I sensed

that the crucial moment had arrived and decided not to allow myself to become ridiculous on any account; I would rather just get a bad mark.

"Have you swallowed this artillery shell?" Kharlampy Diogenovich asked with good-natured curiosity.

He asked the question as naturally as if he had been inquiring whether I had swallowed a plum stone.

"Yes," I said quickly, sensing a trap and deciding to foil his plans with an unexpected answer.

"Then you'd better ask the military instructor to come and dispose of it for you," said Kharlampy Diogenovich, but the form was already laughing.

Sakharov was laughing, and trying to go on looking like the top boy at the same time. Even Shurik Avdeyenko, the gloomiest boy in our form, whom I had saved from certain disaster at the blackboard, was laughing. And Komarov was laughing. Komarov who now called himself Alik but was really Adolf, just as he had always been.

As I looked at him it occurred to me that if we had not had a real gingerhead in our form he would have passed as one because his hair was fair and the freckles that he kept hidden, like his first name, had given themselves away during the injection. But we did have a real gingerhead in the form and Komarov's gingerness had passed unnoticed. And it also occurred to me that if we had not pulled the number of our form off the form-room door a few days ago, the doctor might never have called on us in the first place and nothing would have happened. I began to have vague presentiments of the connection that exists between things and events.

The bell droned funereally through the form's laughter. Kharlampy Diogenovich put a mark against my name in the register and also made a note about me in his notebook.

From then on I took my homework more seriously and never asked the footballers about problems I couldn't solve. Each man to his trade.

Later in life I noticed that nearly everyone is afraid of appearing ridiculous. Particularly women and poets. Perhaps they sometimes appear ridiculous because they are too afraid of appearing so. On the other hand, no one can make someone else look ridiculous as skilfully as a good poet or a good woman.

Of course, it is not very wise to be too afraid of appearing ridiculous, but it is much less wise not to be afraid of ridicule at all.

It seems to me that ancient Rome perished because its emperors in all their marble magnificence failed to realise how ridiculous they were. If they had got themselves some jesters in time (you must hear the truth, if only from a fool), they might have lasted a little longer. But they just went on hoping that the geese would save Rome, and then the Barbarians came and destroyed Rome, its emperors and its geese.

Not that I have any regrets about that, of course. But I do want to express my admiration and gratitude for Kharlampy Diogenovich's method. With the aid of laughter he tempered our sly young hearts and taught us to regard ourselves with a strong enough sense of humour.

FORBIDDEN FRUIT

In accordance with Moslem custom our family never ate pork. Our parents ate none and strictly forbade us to eat any. Although another of Mahomet's precepts — on the subject of alcoholic beverages — was violated, as I now realise, quite unrestrainedly, no liberalism was allowed where pork was concerned.

The ban engendered both an ardent desire and a frigid pride. I dreamed of tasting pork. The smell of roast pork made me dizzy to the point of collapse. I would stand for hours outside shop windows, staring at the glistening sausages with their wrinkled sides and spotted ends. I fancied myself tearing off the skin and plunging my teeth into the succulent, tender meat. I imagined the taste of sausage so clearly that, when I did eventually try it, I was quite surprised to discover how accurately fancy had informed me.

Of course, there had been opportunities of tasting pork at nursery school or when visiting friends but I had never broken the accepted rule.

I can still remember picking the lumps of pork out of a nursery school *pilaf* and giving them away to my friends. The pangs of appetite were overcome by the sweetnees of self-denial. I felt a kind of ideological superiority over my comrades It was satisfying to be something of a mystery to the world at large, as though I had knowledge that no one else possessed. And it made my yearning for the sinful object of desire all the more intense.

There was a nurse who lived in one of the houses in our yard. We called her Auntie Sonya. In those days for some reason we thought of her as a doctor. In general, as one grows up, one notices a steady decline in the status of one's elders.

Auntie Sonya was an elderly lady with her hair cut short and a look of permanent sorrow on her face. She always spoke in a very quiet voice. It was as though she had long since realised that there was nothing in life worth raising one's voice about.

During the communal battles between neighbours that were frequent enough in our yard she scarcely raised her voice at all, which created additional difficulties for her opponents who, having failed to hear what she had said, would lose the thread of the quarrel and be put off their stroke.

Our families were on good terms. Mother told me that Auntie Sonya had saved me from certain death. When I had been struck down by some grave illness, she and mother had taken turns at my bedside for a whole month. For some reason I experienced no feelings of gratitude towards Auntie Sonya for saving me from certain death, but my sense of decorum, when they talked about it, made me glad I was still alive.

She would often come round to sit with us of an evening and tell us her life story, particularly the part about her first husband, who had been killed in the Civil War. I had heard this story many times before and yet I always froze with horror at her description of how she had roamed about among the dead, looking for the body of the man she loved. At this point she would usually begin to cry, and my mother and elder sister would cry with her, then begin comforting her, bring her a glass of water or persuade her to have some tea.

It always astonished me how quickly the women would recover their spirits and soon be able to chatter merrily and even with renewed interest about all kinds of trivial matters. After this she would go home because her husband would be back from work. He was called Uncle Shura.

I was very fond of Uncle Shura. I liked the wild tangle of black hair that hung down over his forehead, his muscular arms with their neatly rolled up sleeves, and even his stoop. It was not the stoop of an office clerk, but the sound, sturdy kind of stance that one finds in some old workmen, although he was neither old nor a workman.

When he came home in the evening he would always set about mending something — table lamps, electric irons, radios and even clocks. All these things were brought to him by neighbours and he repaired them, as a matter of course, free of charge.

Auntie Sonya would sit on the other side of the table, smoke and make gentle fun of him for doing something that was not his business, wasting his time, and so on.

"We'll see whether I'm wasting my time or not," Uncle Shura would mutter indistinctly because he, too, had a cigarette between his teeth. He would turn his next mending job this way and that in his deft, confident hands, blowing off the dust as he did so, and all of a sudden he would look at it from quite a new, unexpected angle.

"Wasting your time and making a fool of yourself," Auntie Sonya would reply and, releasing a haughty stream of smoke from her lips, gloomily wrap her dressing-gown round her.

In the end he would manage to get the clock going, or the radio would start giving out crackles and snatches of music, and he would wink at me and say,

"Well? Was I wasting my time or not?"

I would always rejoice in his success and smile to show that, although it had nothing to do with me, I appreciated being included in his company.

"All right, enough of your boasting," Auntie Sonya would say. "Clear the table and we'll have some tea."

Even in her gruff tone, however, I could detect a secret, deeply hidden note of pride, and I felt glad for Uncle Shura and decided that he was probably just as good as that hero of the Civil War whom Auntie Sonya would never forget.

One evening, when I was sitting with them as usual, my sister dropped in and was invited to stay for tea. Auntie Sonya laid the table, cut some pieces of tender pink bacon fat, put some mustard on the table, and poured out the tea. They had often eaten bacon fat before this, and offered it to me as well, but I had always firmly refused, which for some reason rather amused Uncle Shura. They offered me some now, not very insistently. Uncle Shura placed a few cubes of fat on a piece of bread and held it out to my sister. After a mincing refusal, she accepted this shameful offering and began to eat it. In my indignation I felt the tea that I had begun to drink freeze in my throat, and experienced some difficulty in swallowing it.

"That's the way!" said Uncle Shura. "She's not like you, you little monk!"

I felt how much my sister was enjoying what she ate. I could see it from the way she delicately licked her lips clean of the crumbs of bread defiled by this infidel savoury, and the way she swallowed each piece, sitting foolishly still and pausing as if to listen to what was going on in her mouth and throat. She had started the slice on the side where the thinner pieces of fat lay, and this was a sure sign that she was relishing every morsel, because all normal children, when eating something they like, leave the best piece till last. Clearly she was experiencing enormous pleasure.

Now she was approaching the edge of the slice with the thickest piece of fat on it, systematically intensifying her delight. At the same time, with purely feminine guile she was relating how my brother had jumped out of the window when his form mistress had come round to complain of his conduct. Her story served the dual purpose of distracting attention from what she herself was doing, while subtly flattering me, because everyone knew that my teacher had never been round to complain about me and I certainly had no reason to flee from her through the window.

In the course of her story my sister glanced at me from time to time, trying to discover whether I was still watching her or whether I was so carried away by her tale that I had forgotten what she was doing. But my glance stated quite clearly that I was still keeping her under the most vigilant observation. In reply she opened her eyes very wide as if expressing surprise that I could pay so much attention to a mere trifle. I leered back, alluding vaguely to the retribution that awaited her.

At one moment I thought the time of retribution had

already arrived. My sister choked, then cautiously began to clear her throat. I watched with interest to see what would happen next. Uncle Shura patted her on the back. She blushed and then stopped coughing, indicating that the cure had worked; her embarrassment appeared to be equally shortlived. But I felt that the piece that had stuck in her throat was still there. Pretending to have recovered, she took another bite of bread and bacon fat.

Chew away, I thought to myself. We'll see how you manage to get it down.

But apparently the gods had decided to postpone their vengeance. My sister swallowed this piece safely. In fact, it must also have pushed down the previous piece, because she breathed with relief and became quite cheerful again. Now she ate with redoubled concentration and after each bite licked her lips for so long that it looked almost as if she were showing her tongue at me.

At last she reached the edge of the slice with the thickest piece of fat on it and, before putting it in her mouth, she nibbled away the bread round it, thus building up the pleasure to be gained from the last piece.

Eventually she swallowed this, too, and licked her lips as though reliving the pleasure she had received, and also to show that all evidence of her fall from grace had been destroyed.

The whole thing occupied less time than it takes to tell and could scarcely have been noticed by a casual onlooker. Anyway I am sure neither Uncle Shura nor Auntie Sonya noticed anything.

Having finished her slice, my sister started on her tea, still pretending that nothing out of the ordinary had happened. As soon as she put the cup to her lips I drank my own down very quickly, so that there should be nothing in common between us. Before this I had refused a biscuit because I was determined to make my martyrdom complete and deny myself every possible joy while in her presence. Besides I was slightly offended with Uncle Shura for pressing his food on me less persistently than on my sister. I should not have accepted it, of course, but for her it would have been a good lesson in principle.

In short, my mood was utterly spoiled and, as soon as

I had drunk my tea, I got up to go. They asked me to stay but I was inexorable.

"I must do my homework," I said with the air of the lonely saint granting everyone else complete freedom to indulge in sin.

My sister begged me to stay. She was sure I would denounce her as soon as I got home and she was also afraid of crossing the yard at night by herself.

At home I quickly undressed and got into bed. I was absorbed in envious and gloating contemplation of my sister's apostasy. Strange visions passed through my brain. Now I was a Red partisan captured by the Whites and they were trying to make me eat pork. They tortured me but still I refused. The officers shook their heads in amazement. What a boy! I was amazed at myself but not a morsel passed my lips. They could kill me if they liked, but they wouldn't make me eat.

The door creaked and my sister came in. She at once asked about me.

"He's gone to bed," my mother said. "He seemed rather glum when he came home. Did something happen to him?"

"Oh no, nothing," my sister replied, and came over to my bed. I was afraid she would start arguing and pleading with me and all that kind of thing. Forgiveness was out of the question but I didn't even want her to whittle down the condition I was in. So I pretended to be asleep. She stood over me for a while, then stroked my head gently. But I turned over on to my other side, showing that even while asleep I could tell the hand of a traitor. She stood there a little longer, then withdrew. It seemed to me that she felt some repentance but knew no way of expiating her guilt.

I pitied her a little, but apparently this was a mistake, for only a minute later she began telling mother something in a low voice and they both burst into little fits of laughter, carefully restrained to make it appear that they were afraid of disturbing me. Gradually they calmed down and began to prepare for bed.

Clearly she had enjoyed her evening. She had guzzled bacon fat and I hadn't said anything and, to crown it all, she had made mother laugh. Never mind, I thought, my hour will strike.

Next day the whole family was seated at table, waiting for father to come home for dinner. He arrived late and got angry with mother for making us wait for him. He had been having trouble at work lately and was often gloomy and preoccupied.

It had been my intention to describe my sister's misdeed during the meal, but now I realised this was the wrong time to speak. Nevertheless I glanced at my sister now and then, giving the impression that I was about to launch into an account of her crime. I would actually open my mouth, then say something quite different. As soon as my lips parted she would drop eyes and lower her head in anticipation of the blow. It was even more enjoyable to keep her on the brink of exposure than actually expose her.

One moment her face was pale, the next she would be blushing furiously. Sometimes she would toss her head haughtily, then immediately her imploring eyes would beg forgiveness for this rebellious gesture. She had no appetite and pushed away the plate of soup almost untouched. Mother urged her to finish it.

"Of course, she doesn't want it," I said. "She ate so much yesterday at Uncle Shura's."

"So much what?" my brother asked, missing everything as usual.

Mother looked at me anxiously and shook her head, without letting father see. My sister took the plate back and began eating her soup in silence. Now I was really enjoying myself. I transferred a boiled onion from my plate to hers. Boiled onion was the bugbear of our childhood. We all hated it. Mother gave me a severe glance of inquiry.

"She likes onions," I said. "You do, don't you?" I added fondly to my sister.

Her only response was to bow her head even lower over the plate.

"If you like them, you can have mine as well," said my brother, scooping one up in his spoon. He was just about to put it on her plate, but my father gave him

64

such a look that the spoon stopped in midair and beat a cowardly retreat.

Between the first and second courses I devised a fresh amusement. I dressed a slice of bread with little rings of cucumber from the salad and began nibbling delicately at my vegetarian sandwich, pretending now and then to dissolve with pleasure. This, I thought, was a very clever way of reconstructing the scene of my sister's shameful fall. She stared at me in astonishment, as though the pantomime meant nothing to her or, at least, nothing shameful. Further than this, however, her protest did not go.

In other words, dinner was a tremendous success. Virtue blackmailed ruthlessly and wickedness hung its head. After dinner we drank tea. Father became noticeably more cheerful, and so, accordingly, did we. My sister was particularly gay. The colour flooded into her cheeks and her eyes sparkled. She started relating some incident that had occurred at school, constantly appealing to me as a witness, as though nothing had happened between us. I felt slightly disgusted by this familiarity. It struck me that a person with her past could have behaved with a little more modesty instead of jumping into the limelight. She could have waited until other, more worthy people thought fit to relate that story. I was about to administer a moderate dose of punishment, but father unwrapped a newspaper and took out a packet of new exercise books.

In those pre-war years exercise books were as hard to come by as textiles and certain foods. These were the best, glossy kind, with margins, clearly marked in red, and heavy, cool pages of a bluish white colour, like milk.

There were nine of these exercise books altogether and father gave us three each. I at once felt my high spirits begin to wane. Such egalitarianism seemed to me the limit of injustice.

I was doing well at school, and sometimes came top in one subject or another. In fact, our relatives and friends were told that I was getting excellent marks in all subjects, perhaps in order to balance the impression created by my brother's unfortunate notoriety.

He was considered a very energetic slacker. As his teacher put it, his ability to judge his own actions lagged

5—1126

far behind his temperament. I imagined that temperament of his in the shape of a mischievous little imp that was always running on ahead of my brother and that he could never catch up with. Perhaps, it was to help him in this chase that ever since the age of eleven he had dreamed of becoming a driver. On every available scrap of paper he would scribble an application he had read somewhere:

To the Director of Transport

I request you to employ me in the organisation of which you are in charge because I am a qualified driver, 3rd grade.

Later he succeeded in realising this fervent ambition. The organisation of which a certain director was in charge entrusted him with a vehicle, but it turned out that catching up with his temperament entailed exceeding the speed limit, and in the end he had to change his profession.

And here was I, almost an outstanding pupil, being reduced to the same level as my brother, who, starting from the back page as usual, would fill up these beautiful exercise books with his idiotic applications.

And to the same level as my sister, who only the day before had been guzzling bacon fat and was today receiving a present which she had done nothing whatever to deserve.

I pushed aside the exercise books and sat scowling at the table, painfully aware of the humiliating tears of resentment welling up in my throat. My father tried to talk me round and promised to take me fishing in the mountains, but it was no use. The more they tried to console me the more strongly I felt that I had been unjustly passed over.

"Look! I've got two blotters!" my sister sang out all of a sudden, as she opened one of the exercise books. This was the last straw. Perhaps, if fate had not granted her that extra sheet of blotting paper, what did happen might never have happened.

I stood up and in a trembling voice said to my father:

"Yesterday, she was eating bacon fat..."

An indecent silence descended on the room. With a sense of fear I realised that I had done something wrong.

66

Either I had not expressed myself quite clearly or else there was too close a connection between Mahomet's great laws and the sneaking desire to lay hands on someone else's excercise books.

Father stared at me gravely from under his slightly swollen lids. Slowly his eyes filled with fury. I realised that his gaze held nothing for me to look forward to. I made one more pitiful attempt to correct the situation and channel his fury in the right direction.

"She ate bacon fat yesterday at Uncle Shura's," I said desperately, feeling that my whole case was collapsing.

The next moment father seized me by the ears, shook my head and, as though realising it would not come off, lifted me up and threw me to the floor. In the brief seconds before I landed I felt a stab of pain and heard the creak of my ears stretching.

"Son of a bitch!" he cried. "On top of everything else am I to have traitors in my own house!"

He grabbed his leather jacket and swung out of the room, giving the door such a slam that plaster fell off the walls. I remember being shaken not so much by the pain or by what he said, but by the expression of utter repugnance with which he had seized my ears. It was the expression of someone about to kill a snake.

Stunned by what had happened, I remained lying on the floor for a long time. My mother tried to lift me up while my brother, in a state of wild excitement, ran round me in circles, pointing at my ears and roaring delightedly.

"Our top boy!"

I was very fond of my father and this was the first time he had punished me.

Many years have passed since then. For a long time now I have been eating the pork that is available to all, though I don't think I am any the happier for it. But the lesson was not wasted. It taught me for the rest of my life that no lofty principle can justify meanness and treachery, and that all treachery is the hairy caterpillar that grows from a small envy, no matter under what high principles it may be concealed.

THE LETTER

When I was fifteen I received a letter with a passionate declaration of love. I still have the impression that those words which blazed out at me as I read them were not written in ordinary blue ink, but inscribed in burnished gold. Just before the postwoman handed me the letter, I had been running down the outside steps of our two-storey house holding piece of electric cable. The aim of the exercise was to see whether I could endure the mysterious force of the electric current passing through my body. With the bare wire touching the metal railing of the steps, I raced down as fast as I could, emitting a trail of bright blue sparks.

A storm the night before had snapped the cable. Most of the deadly current had been spent on the roof of our house. Now I was amusing myself with the bits of electricity that remained.

It was spring-time. The ornate railings were entwined with even more ornate glycinia blossom. Heavy bunches hung from the outer side. They were as blue as the electric sparks flying from under my hand.

Near the middle of the first flight of steps was a landing which led to the communal W. C.

From time to time the inmates of our house would make their way towards it. As soon as they touched the railings, I placed the naked cable on the metal. This usually made them yell out or leap silently onto the landing in a wild bound, but whatever the reaction, none of them changed their destination.

I read the letter, still clutching the cable in one hand. Then realising at once that this game was needed no longer, that its end had come, most likely forever, I threw the cable away and ran into the house.

Although the letter was unsigned, I guessed straight-away who had written it. It was a girl who had been in the same class as me two years ago. Then we had been separated when the school was split up into one for boys and one for girls like the old grammar schools. I hadn't seen her or thought about her since then. My name had been next to hers in the class register. Not only were we next to each other, but we even had the same initials. Such a coincidence could not pass unnoticed. Even then we had both sensed that it was more than chance. And now at last this letter.

The gold letters blazed and danced on the paper. I read the missive through several times, gratefully fell in love with its author and then tore it into small pieces and threw it in the dustbin.

My actions were motivated by the strong patriarchal shame and unconscious logic of the budding socialist. I could describe the course of this logic now roughly as follows: the letter I had received was happiness, and you should feel ashamed to be happy, just as you should feel ashamed to be well-fed among the starving. But since it is hard to renounce happiness (tactics!), you must conceal it, that is, keep it in your head and destroy all the material evidence.

Now I roamed the streets in the hope of meeting her. I did not have a very clear idea what I would do when I met her. Well, of course, I'll have to go up to her first, I thought, then as soon as a convenient opportunity presents itself, I'll offer her my heart and my life, to the day I die, naturally.

I can't say I was in any great hurry to see her. As with all budding socialists, the main thing for me was the programme, and this had been outlined with exquisite clarity in her missive. As far as everything else was concerned, there was a whole life-time for that, and at fifteen life seems immense. However much of it you waste, you don't know what to do with the rest, and it froths over in abundance.

Then one day, when I was standing with my friends in the main street of our town, Generalissimo Street, to be more precise, she walked past us with two girlfriends.

I had time to notice the inspired pallor of her flushed cheek, her quick gait and slim figure. In the last two years she had changed from a girl into a young woman, still managing to stay as slim as she was in the seventh form, so crucial for our class.

In short, I saw before me that spring of pale-pink radiance so vital for the first tender feelings of a boy of my age.

The trick Nature plays in this case, however, is that every boy who goes through this stage or, to be more accurate, receives this vaccination, this injection of love fever, interprets this radiance as a special favour of fate, which has sensed the need of his delicate heart and one day, with perfect tact, with the sensitivity of a Japanese landscape gardener, combines all the rare qualities of his fragile and capricious ideal in a single girl.

Seeing her blushing cheek, I knew for certain that my guess was right and realised that going up to her would not be that simple. Although we had managed to exchange only one swift glance, it was somehow decided in that instant that to recognise and greet each other now, two years later, would be embarrassing, particularly as the secret of the letter now lay between us.

No, no! she cried to me with this fleeting glance. Not now, not here, because if you say hello to me now, it will mean you have told your friends about my letter, and I shall die of shame.

Now I began to see her more and more. Sometimes she was with her elder sister, sometimes with a crowd of girlfriends and boys I didn't know, and I felt that each time it was getting harder for me to go up to her.

Her sister had also been in the same class as us, by the way, although she was a year or two older, I don't remember how this happened, but it probably wasn't through any excessive love of learning. To be quite consistent I stopped saying hello to the sister too, which she seemed not to notice. She was a sleepy sort of girl and although more attractive then her younger sister to look at, with her heavy delicate eyelids, limpid face and bright lips, you could tell the boys were attracted by the younger one. Because she, the younger one, exuded a kind of restlessness, an impatient expectation of life's enjoyments which infected those around her.

In short, it was getting harder and harder to go up to her.

I was waiting for the right romantic moment and was actually not in a great hurry to get to know her. I thought there was no need to hurry, now that my life was dedicated to her and her alone.

In the meantime an army fellow, with the rank of captain, as my friends eagerly informed me, began to appear by her side together with the other boys and girls.

And now I noticed that if the captain was with her my beloved seemed to get embarrassed and avoid my glance when we met. I took her embarrassment as infinitely moving proof of her love, pleasantly flattering my pride, but perhaps excessively strong.

And now, by darting her meaningful glances, I tried to convey to her that she shouldn't be too embarrassed about her captain, for she and I both knew what a great secret united us, that he, poor fellow, had never received a letter like that and, judging by his advanced years, probably never would.

The captain was a lad of about twenty-seven, an age which then seemed to me far too elderly for love.

It is possible that my secret love interpreted my glances correctly, because with time, she almost ceased to be embarrassed when I met her with the captain, and sometimes curved her lips in the hint of a smile, which I easily explained as a necessary stratagem. How could she, poor thing, love one person and endure the attentions of another, I thought.

Thus in this state of blessed imbecility, accompanying my beloved from time to time like an invisible shadow, I existed until the middle of the summer when she and her sister began to go dancing in the town park with the captain.

Under the influence of the music in the park my feelings, I recall, became soured by a certain bitterness.

The post-war dancing floor shuffled to captured German and Russian music. In the crowd of dancers I would glimpse her pale face, lifted enquiringly up to the captain. A tall, well-built fellow, he gazed down at her genially and, blast him, with a faint air of condescension which I found insulting.

It would be hard to imagine anything more ghastly than a dance floor in those days. I can still see it now — the ageing spinsters who circle for years on this small piece of asphalt, as with each dance something feminine, human, seems to splash out of them until they have fashioned that professional mask with the hungry hollow eyes. And the slick guys, and the elderly criminals who have now taken up more peaceful occupations but come here for sentimental reasons and, finally, the inevitable first dancer, who works like a water-carrier, dancing the then very fashionable shimmy and rolling his eyes in coiffeured ecstasy!

Suddenly at the edge of the dance floor or somewhere near the middle a tiny whirlpool of fisticuffs would appear, gradually drawing more and more people into its vortex, with whistles, shouts and girls running away wildly.

Shame for all this wretchedness and fear for my beloved and also for myself. Anxiety together with a cheap curiosity to see the fighting and blood, and at the same time a constant feeling of being debased by the excessive dose of vulgarity in everything that was happening here, and also the need to hide this aggravation, to twist my lips into the smile of a lad who knows more than he says and yet says more than those around him are worth.

But the worse thing is the disgraceful price put on your personality as soon as you come in here. It is as if you have cheapened yourself to a great extent already, yet still not enough, and you are complaining about it, and nobody either wants to or can listen to you, because you are complaining to yourself. But your face obviously shows signs of displeasure and by these signs you could be denounced at any moment as a cripple, as someone incapable from birth of beating up a defenceless person with a gang, or of playing a dirty trick on some unsuspecting jerk or his girl and in general of behaving like a shit when you're sure you can get away with it, and sometimes not quite sure, but better if you are.

All these emotions churned inside me for many days as I watched her on the dance floor. At last one of my friends practically threw me onto the bench where she was sitting with her sister and the captain after a dance.

Giggling with embarrassment, I introduced myself and began explaining that I had been in the same class as her and her sister two years ago in School No. 2, the one between the stadium and the church, although neither of them could have forgotten where it was for the simple reason that they still went there (it was the boys who had been moved to another school).

No did I forget to mention that when we were in the same class our surnames and first names began with the same letter.

While I was talking, she lifted her head several times and her face lit up and then went blank again, but her eyes begged me not to make a scene. She kept turning to her captain and touching his chest gently, reassuring him with this light affectionate gesture and keeping him at a distance from our reminiscences.

I forgot to mention that during this monologue of mine when our eyes met I tried to indicate as eloquently as possible by my expression that never, under any circumstances whatsoever, would anyone, particularly him (then followed a romantic swiveling of the eyes in his direction) learn of the existence of the great letter. And my confused monologue itself with the detailed description of the location of our school was also intended to persuade the captain that we had neither written nor even spoken to each other since.

It must be said that the captain, who realised as soon as I began talking that I was not some importunate lout, behaved towards me in a most genial fashion.

"Kostya," he said simply and gave me a firm, comradely shake of the hand when she introduced us.

A little later he even went off to dance with her sister, leaving us alone for two or three dances.

What bliss it was to sit down on the bench beside her, see in close proximity her charming profile with the snub nose and long neck and inhale the fragrant perfume, which was all the more intoxicating because then and for a long time afterwards I took it to be the natural odour of the fine radiant youthfulness.

Three of my friends walked past us several times demonstratively. You could see from their faces that they were offended by my happiness. When our eyes met, I sent them smiles such as a person suddenly borne aloft to exquisite but very insecure heights might send to earth. They replied to these smiles with looks that advised me to come down forthwith from those ridiculous heights and discuss with them what had happened. In persuading me to go up to her they had obviously expected a more comic effect.

Finally one of them, the one who had pushed me over to the bench and evidently therefore felt most responsible for my behaviour, came up to us and after a somewhat stiff apology to my companion, took me aside.

He was an evacuee from Leningrad, and we thought, and he readily agreed with us, that he had retained the cool genteel polish of the typical Petersburgian. We walked off some ten paces.

"I must tell you that you look a perfect idiot," he said, looking at me sternly.

I remembered that he was the one who had taken me up to her. Everything had worked out so simply and marvellously that suddenly, quite unexpectedly for myself and even more so for him, of course, I embraced him. He shook himself free indignantly and went off to join the others. I watched him go. Tall and thin, he walked with the precise gait of an envoy.

It never even occurred to me to blackmail her with the letter, but now that we were alone I thought I must hint that the missive had reached its destination and that the great act of union between our souls had taken place in all its beauty and selflessness.

"Oh, do tear it up!" she said at the mention of the letter, touching my shirt lightly with her fingers. "I was so silly then..."

"Never!" I exclaimed vehemently, putting all the fervour of my feelings into the word.

I wanted to say that the feelings which her letter had aroused were forever and now nothing could be changed,

74

so this deception was the most striking form of truth. She sighed and withdrew her hand.

For some reason I gave a triumphant look at the captain, who was now returning to the bench, holding her sister by the elbow, something which I had not yet mastered, incidentally.

From then onwards we often met and spent the evening together. For some reason it was always in a foursome.

I knew perfectly well that the captain was interested in her and not her sister, but did not feel any jealousy or sense of rivalry. That was impossible, just as it is impossible to be jealous of someone who sits down by a bonfire next to you and stretches out his hands to the heat. Or, to be more precise, if one is to continue the comparison, you yourself come out of the rainy night to this fire, by which he is already sitting, stirring his simple love broth in his old soldier's mess-tin. So it is he, not you, who moves aside to give you a place by the fire, still stirring his broth, by the way. And what difference does it make that you noticed the fire before he did, or rather, that it noticed you and even winked at you from afar with its tongues of flame,— now you can both warm yourselves by it, and there is nothing wrong with that.

Thus I reasoned, taking the temporary balance of power for harmony. Sooner or later rivalry or something of the sort was bound to rear its ugly head. And so it did.

It seemed quite natural that during our joint outings all the minor travelling expenses, for cold drinks, ice-creams, visiting the park and sometimes the cinema, although very rarely, the captain immediately took upon himself.

In the early days I used to tender my solitary rouble on such occasions, but he and she thrust it back into my hand so firmly that I soon stopped paying any attention to this, since there is nothing people take for granted so quickly as other people paying for them.

One day, when he was getting some grape juice for our joint beloved and I was standing unobtrusively nearby with her sister, he nodded in our direction and said: "Come on, kids. Charlie's paying."

It sounded a bit rude. I am now quite sure that he didn't

mean to offend or humiliate me with this joke, but at the time I felt a burning shame and for the first time hatred for this nice lad.

One thing was that I simply couldn't refuse, foreseeing the unwise and awkward consequences of such a refusal, particularly because the juice had already been poured into four glasses and, which was most surprising, I still wanted to drink it, even more than before, in fact.

Another thing was that when he made this joke about being a sugar-daddy, I saw her smile into her glass, and it was a rather sarcastic smile. This really upset me, and afterwards I often remembered this smile until I decided there actually hadn't been a smile at all. It was the effect of the light passing through the glass and the juice that had given her lips that treacherous curl.

But perhaps the worst thing was that we had already agreed to go to the cinema and, as luck would have it, I had no money on me. Now, after what had happened, I simply couldn't let him pay for my ticket. But to refuse outright seemed somehow embarrassing and pointless, because if I did I would have to leave them, and I didn't want to do that.

Of course, it had occurred to me before that I shouldn't take advantage of his generosity, although, I repeat, the sums involved were fairly small. But in the dizzy state of blissful intoxication, in which I had been ever since I went up to them that day and we began going out together, I had somehow come to regard all this as a male favour. You pay today and I'll pay tomorrow, although this tomorrow kept being put off to some unforeseeable future.

I was also aware of another way of looking at the situation, which I had deliberately not thought out fully, sensing that it was not a very worthy one. Nevertheless it occasionally presented itself in vague outline to my inner eye, and I cannot keep silent about it now. To put it in a nutshell, I thought, and had possibly begun to think so some time before, that she and I were doing him a kind of favour by admitting him to our company, in return for which he was repaying us by meeting these trifling expenses.

Of course, if we are going to continue the comparison with the bonfire, I was not jealous of him for sitting by my fire. But I knew, blast it, that the fire was burning for me, that the wonderful letter had perhaps been written with a burning twig snatched from this very fire!

That she could not write such a letter or indeed any love letter to another, I not only did not doubt, but was quite sure that anyone who had written a letter like that would spend the rest of their days serving it faithfully, as long as they had the strength to live up to it, and would never think of anything else.

Then suddenly that careless remark about a sugar-daddy who treats everybody. On the way between the kiosk and the summer cinema where we were going, I kept wondering how to evade his new act of charity without losing face, and couldn't think of anything.

In those post-war days lots of films captured in Germany were shown in our cinemas. As a rule, they were operas or pastoral stories with endless songs or clumsy reviews with lots of smiling "girls", broad-bottomed and hefty as Friesian cows, if that's what Friesian cows are like, of course.

Many years later I came to the conclusion that these films represented nothing but the tastes of the rulers of the Reich.

It was one of these films that we were about to see. The film was called *Never Forget Me* and starred the fat, dulcet-voiced Gigli in the main role. Like any inhabitant of a provincial town, I knew all about the picture from hearsay, although I hadn't seen it yet. I must admit that I liked Gigli's voice, especially if you didn't pay too much attention to the screen as you listened to him.

We were close to the cinema now and I realised with horror that in about ten minutes time I would suffer yet another humiliation, which I just couldn't face, so I began to run down the film. It was the art of the fat cats, after all, and in order to run it down, in those conditions particularly, you did not need any great oratory or fine arguments.

For this film I went on to criticise all those captured pictures in general with their sickening sentimentality.

The more I panned the picture, the more stubbornly

my beloved pouted. At that time I didn't know it was as dangerous to try and stop a woman on her way to a place of entertainment as the Roman mob on the road to the Coliseum.

When I switched from *Never Forget Me* to all captured German films in general, she suddenly asked me:

"You study German, don't you?"

"Yes, so what?" I retorted.

I thought she had seen some contradiction between my criticism of German films and my study of the German language. But her question was prompted by something else.

"Talk to Kostya," she suggested, never dreaming what a genie she had let out of the bottle. "He spent two years in Germany."

"Sprechen Sie Deutsch?" I howled with delight, like a pure-blooded German who had suddenly met a fellow-countryman after being held captive by the Polynesians for many years.

"Natürlich," he replied dejectedly, somewhat taken aback by my enthusiasm.

After that you just couldn't stop me. In those days I learnt languages with the greatest of ease, which is why I still don't know a single one properly. I had been studying German for two years and could already make myself understood to the prisoners-of-war who used to praise my pronunciation, probably in return for the cigarettes I gave them *(Prima Deutsch!)*.

Studying a foreign language you reach a state of delirium, when you start babbling it fluently in your sleep, although you still stumble over it when you are awake, and when every object you see has its foreign double, in short, the time arrives when your inflamed brain overcomes a kind of incompatibility barrier between the two languages. This was the state I was in then.

I was crammed full of German proverbs, genteel phrases from pre-revolutionary teach-yourself books, antifascist slogans, aphorisms from Marx and Goethe, and abbreviated texts designed to develop the student's vigilance against possible German spies (which seemed to assume that the spies would suddenly lose their nerve

78

and start talking to the locals in German). In addition to this I knew by heart several patriotic Russian songs directed against the occupying troops and translated into German, as well as some German classical poetry.

All this burst out of me with a menacing force at this unfortunate moment.

"So you speak German, do you?" I asked, turning to him and not even trying to shorten my step as we gradually approached the cinema at the beginning of the next block. *"Wunderbar!"* I continued. "Did you study it on your own or at college? Oh, I understand, you learnt it when you were in Germany as an officer in the Allied army. Not as a prisoner-of-war, I hope? No, no, I was joking, of course. Karl Marx said the best test of knowing a language is being able to understand humour in it, and that knowledge of foreign languages is a weapon in the struggle for life."

I looked at Kostya and sensed that he could hardly understand anything. Now and then his face lit up as he recognised a familiar word and tried to hang on to it, but then a stream of new words rushed up and swept it away.

I felt triumphant. The cinema was very close now. The faint murmur of the crowd wafted through the trees and bushes. Now people were asking passersby if they had a spare ticket. At the sight of them I almost jumped for joy.

My beloved bit her lip. The loudspeaker over the cinema entrance was playing the popular "Tales from the Vienna Woods."

"The sunset on the Rhine," I said, turning to the captain, "is as beautiful as the sunrise in the Swiss Alps... These pheasants are from our family forest. *Probieren Sie, bitte!* My huntsman is a very strange chap."

At this point I gestured at the crown of one of the camphor trees under which we were walking. My companions looked up in amazement...

"Know you the land where the lemon trees bloom?" I asked the captain, as usual not knowing where to stop and going too far.

The captain said nothing.

"Why don't you answer him, Kostya?" our beloved asked hastily when I stopped to get my breath back. She was offended on his behalf.

"Why interrupt?" Kostya replied calmly. "I wish I could spout stuff like that in the exams..."

That autumn Kostya was going to take the entrance exams for a military academy in Leningrad. We went up to the cinema. Kostya walked around trying to find some spare tickets, but without success. I rejoiced, but too hastily and, more important, too openly.

Half an hour later we were back by the dance floor in the park. They had gone to dance as usual, leaving her sister and me sitting on a bench.

Then, as now, I was a bad dancer. The rhythms went astray somewhere in my torso and reached my legs in the form of vague, retarded jerks. So naturally her sister was in no hurry to dance with me. She just sat beside me, and we talked about something or, which was even better, were silent. Very occasionally she was asked to dance, rarely because frequenters of the dance floor took her to be my girl.

And so we sat there, quite unsuspectingly, this evening as well. First one dance finished, then a second and a third, but still there was no sign of them.

"Where can they be?" I said, looking at her sister.

"How should I know?" she replied, shrugging her shoulders and looking at me with her sleepy eyes under the delicate eyelids.

"Let's go and have a look," I nodded towards the dance floor.

"If you like," she said with another shrug of the shoulders and got up from the bench.

We walked round the jostling circle of the dance floor. I looked for her among the dancing couples and realised they were not there. A nauseating depression swept over me.

"Perhaps they're in the shooting-gallery?" I said uncertainly.

She shrugged her shoulders, and we went into the shooting-gallery.

It was empty. Leaning with his back against the counter and looking in the mirror, the man in charge was firing bullet after bullet at the target from an air-gun. He had just scored his fourth bull's-eye.

"Wanna go?" he said, scoring a fifth bull's-eye without turning round. "I'll fire with one hand and you can fire with two. How about it?"

"No, thanks," I said, watching him score his fifth bull's-eye.

We went up to the cold drinks pavilion, but they weren't there either. It occurred to me that while we had been looking for them they might have returned to the bench and be waiting for us. I made her hurry back to our usual spot, but they weren't there. So I decided to wait for them. But they still did not come. Suddenly I had a nasty suspicion. Say they were all plotting against me. Staring at my companion's face, I tried to detect a hint of concealed mockery, but could see nothing of the kind. Just the sleepy, limpid face with beautiful eyes under heavy lids. I couldn't even make out whether their disappearance worried her or not.

"Perhaps they're over there?" I nodded towards the depths of the park.

She shrugged her shoulders silently, and we began to search the park, investigating every bench in every remote corner. We even went behind the statue of Stalin, in case they were sitting on the top step of the pedestal, leaning cosily against the hem of his granite greatcoat. But they weren't there either.

Eventually we reached the most secluded section of the park, where you could hear faint music, strained of its brash vulgarity by the leaves and needles of the trees. We walked over to a bench under a box-tree, although you could see perfectly well even from a distance that there was no one on it. But for some reason I suddenly had to go up to that shady bench, to make absolutely sure, perhaps... So we went up and stood there. A clump of pampas grass was growing next to it. For some reason I lifted up the drooping grass, pulled it back and looked under it as if the two of them might have suddenly fallen off the bench and rolled under the clump.

"No sign," I said and let go of the grass which rustled strangely.

I looked at my companion. She shrugged her shoulders. And suddenly I became acutely aware of it all, this secluded part of the park, the faint music and the grown-up innocent girl with the heavy lids and bright lips. My head began to go round. I put my hands on her shoulders and felt the shadow of a great and sad thought flit over me and dissappear.

"Where can they be?" I asked, trying to return to my strange state of a moment before. But obviously she too sensed that something in me had changed.

"How should I know?" she said, shrugging her shoulders, which could have been interpreted as a weak attempt to free herself.

I removed my hands.

The thought which had come to me in that instant was so staggering that I said nothing for the rest of the evening and after seeing my companion home around midnight continued to reflect upon it.

When I put my hands on the girl's shoulders, saw close up the beautiful sleepy eyes under their heavy lids and sensed that I could kiss her, I suddenly realised to my amazement that at that moment my love had strayed from its intended course and was now flowing almost painlessly into an unexpected side channel. Then I became aware of, even as it were saw, the variety of life in general and, consequently, of my own life and love.

And at the same time I had the feeling, like a sad presentiment, that at all its noblest moments life would reveal itself to me in all its variety and that I would never be able to take advantage of any of its many branches, but would always tread the designated path... Because so many branches are no good to us. Just give us what is unique and original. For that we're quite happy if our brains are bashed in and our hearts beaten up. Variety's no good to us. Variety's a pain in the neck, and we wouldn't lift a finger or cock an ear for it.

I am, as it were, developing this idea now, yet it occurred to me for the first time on that delightful, but ill-starred evening.

I don't remember how they explained their disappearance, and so I prefer not to invent anything; they must have explained it somehow and I believed them because I wanted to. In any case, we continued to meet now and then. Sometimes I began to despair, but my native optimism and the memory of the unforgettable letter always prevailed in the end.

Yet there were many bitter moments when it seemed that all was lost, that there had never been any letter and I had simply dreamed it all up.

One day in my presence when she was talking to her sister and reminiscing about when we were all the same class, she suddenly said:

"Remember what he was like then and look what he's like now..."

This was said with a kind of quiet regret. The insult made me turn cold, but I said nothing. After all you can't prove that today you're better than yesterday and tomorrow you'll be better than today, although I wanted to very badly. When I came home that evening, I stared hopelessly for a long time in the mirror at my sallow face, pinched from a bout of malaria.

Nevertheless the scales gradually tipped in my favour. With each meeting I began to notice thankfully secret signs of her attention. The poor captain had completely faded into the background. All the last week we had met in a threesome. He had disappeared, obviously realising that he was beginning to look ridiculous. Supremely tactful, I did not ask about him and even pretended not to be aware of my victory.

At last the one and only evening arrived, when there were just the two of us. I rejoiced. To be honest, I had always been sure that this evening would come sooner or later. It represented the victory of refined theory over the simple practice of the captain, who was actually not such a bad chap, after all.

But what can you do, if you've never received a letter like that. Just mind your own business. Mind your own business, dear captain, don't go throwing your money around and don't make fun of someone who, before embarking on this stormy voyage, received something devilishly like a pilot's chart by post.

It was evening. We stood by the gate of her house. She was wearing a fabulous blue dress that shimmered round her slim figure. From the windows of her house shone a faint light turned green by the vine leaves of the summer-house. Together with the light came the hum of voices and laughter. Now and then the scent of ripening grapes wafted over like a light breeze.

I stood before her and felt the first kiss ripen in the semi-darkness. With a kind of astronomical slowness and inevitability my face approached hers which was shining in the dusk. She gave me a long, sweet, searching and, I also sensed, enquiring look.

I was terribly excited not only by the prospect of the miracle close at hand, but also by the fear of its scandalous consequences. I could not make out whether she realised what was maturing at that moment.

She just gave me this long look, and I felt waves of courage and timidity sweep over me in turn.

"Your face keeps changing all the time," she whispered in surprise.

"Does it?" I whispered back, although I could feel that it was changing, but hadn't thought she could see it.

I was glad she had noticed the power of my emotion. I had time to think that if she were overcome by shame or repulsion when I kissed her, I would try to explain that I did not realise what I was doing.

The pale oval of her face was very close now. The terrible moment of entering the warm cloud was imminent.

"Don't do that," I heard the provocating whisper as I buried my lips in the shattering (with childhood or primeval memories perhaps?) milky fragrance of her cheek.

The breathtaking eternity passed, and I felt the fragrant cloudiness of the first touches slowly recede and the sensation grew gradually dry and sweet, perhaps too sweet...

But then she slipped away through the gate and vanished into the darkness. All I could hear was her heels clicking on the path up to the house, then tapping on the porch steps, and suddenly she appeared in the lighted porch, knocked at the door and, bending down quickly so that I could see lock of hair fall over her eyes, peeped into the post-box.

I looked at her, intoxicated by what had happened and surprised by the soberness of her movements: what letter could she be expecting now, after the one she had sent and particularly after what had just happened? She waited a few moments for someone to open the door. I watched her and suddenly felt so extraordinarily strong, that I was sure she would turn round in my direction if I willed her to.

For a few moments I gazed at her rapturously from afar, trying to will her to do as I wanted and sure that I would succeed. But then the door opened and she slipped inside without looking back.

Quite undeterred by this, I returned home along the quiet outlying streets lined with small houses and gardens. Behind each garden fence I was greeted by the fierce yapping of a dog which accompanied me as far as the next garden where another custodian awaited me, yelping impatiently. The dogs were handing me on like a baton.

I took no notice of them. I was full of the confidence of a man or, rather, an alchemist, who after many failures has at last had his first miraculous success. I felt all-powerful. I stopped by a fence behind which there was a particularly ferocious dog. Barking fit to choke, she was pawing up the earth and kicking it aside with her hind legs.

Squatting down I looked through the fence at her eyes full of senseless spite and informed her out loud that goodness and love were all-powerful and that if I wanted to I could make her stop barking and give friendly licks and yaps instead, because now I even loved her, the stupid thing. The dog must really have been stupid, because my words made no impression on her whatever and she went on barking like mad.

The next day I walked along the seashore, still under the impression of our meeting, remembering all the breathtaking details and, most important, feeling twice the man I had been before.

Our next meeting was to take place the following day. Although the day before I had begged her to see me today, she had refused, saying she had things to do at home.

Now I felt that it wasn't a bad thing to have a day's rest.

I strolled along the seashore going over in my mind the countless riches of our last meeting. The day was sunny and not yet very hot. Suddenly I happened to meet Kostya, who was also taking a walk on his own. We greeted each other, and I shook his hand more firmly than usual, thereby trying to convey my sincere compassion and hope that he would bear this adversity like a man. I felt him shake my hand more firmly than usual as well, and suddenly realised that he must have guessed what had happened and was now silently congratulating me on my well-deserved victory. Such high-mindedness amazed me, and I gave his hand an even firmer shake. I decided that he had been to see her and she had told him all.

"Have you been to her place?" I asked.

"No," he said. "I've just arrived back from manoeuvres and I'm going away again today."

"Where?"

"To Leningrad," he said, giving me a slightly puzzled look. "Didn't she tell you?"

"She must have forgotten," I replied, looking him straight in the eye, if my memory serves me right.

The news came as a bolt from the blue. By a great effort of will I managed to stop the blood rushing to my face.

"She's coming to see me off today," he added in an excessively casual tone.

We went on walking along the seashore. I think he asked me to have a last meal with him, but I could neither hear nor understand anything properly and said goodbye at the first convenient opportunity.

So that was what my victory meant! I had simply occupied a place that had been temporarily vacated! I began to go over our recent meetings day by day and realised that the increasing warmth in our relationship, the secret signs of attention and, finally, the breathtaking rendezvous, were explained by the fact that he was going away.

I had known all the time that he was going to study at the academy, of course, but for some reason I had thought it would be much later, at the end of August, and secondly, I had never dreamed that my victory could be connected with the mechanical removal of a rival. All this seemed quite intolerable now.

Walking along Port Street on Saturday evening, I caught sight of her and her sister in a crowd of other girls. Custom demanded that I should go up to her.

She was wearing the same light blue shimmering dress, but now it looked somewhat snake-like to me. We nodded at each other, but I did not go over. We continued to stay with our respective companies, I with my friends and she with hers.

She obviously decided that I was embarrassed by her friends, so she and her sister dropped behind them a bit. But I still did not go over. With a bitter pleasure I noticed traces of what I then took to be confusion or panic on her face. Her sister, who seemed to have finally woken up, looked at me with a respectful curiosity.

My friends, who now knew all about it, gave me benevolent looks, as if I had given away to the needy some vain riches bestowed upon me by fortune and had now returned to my poor, but honest companions.

In the end her sister called me over. She herself was standing by the parapet dividing off the beach. She was looking out to sea. I went up, and she turned slightly towards me.

"What's happened?" she asked, staring cautiously into my eyes.

"Has Kostya gone?" I asked, expecting her to get embarrassed.

For some reason she was not embarrassed in the slightest.

"Yes," she said, "he sent his regards."

"Thanks," I said with theatrical dignity and added: "But I don't need any rendezvous that has been stolen from him."

It was a carefully prepared and, I thought, quite devastating remark.

"So you're like that..." she whispered with her lips alone, as if suddenly aware of her fatal blunder.

Then she turned quickly and began to walk away, her sad, sweet head drooping, faster and faster, like all women trying to leave behind the tears that are welling up.

I longed to rush after her, but restrained myself. The town had become sad and empty, and I went home.

That evening I got tonsillitis, and by the time I recovered a week later, the break was no longer so painful.

Incidentally, one of my friends, as I later discovered, always got ill whenever he fell in love. And the gravity of the illness was in direct proportion to the intensity of his feelings, ranging from high fever to flu.

Never again did I see the girl who had sent me that marvellous letter. I think her parents sold their house that year and moved to another town.

While we were going out together it sometimes occurred to me that she could not have written such an ardent missive herself. Perhaps she copied it from an old-fashioned novel, adding a few words of her own, I thought. I did not find the idea in the least offensive. I believed she had sent me a sign, a precise hieroglyph, of her state. And who had invented the hieroglyph was not that important.

But on the other hand, who knows? Perhaps her feelings gave her just enough inspiration to write the letter. At all events, it is a secret which I have no intention of trying to unravel, nor do I intend to listen to third-party's interpretations, however perceptive or even flattering to the narrator's pride they may be.

MY IDOL

He used to sit in front of me in class, so during lessons I would admire the manly shape of the back of his head and his broad shoulders. I think it was that indomitable back of his head that I liked first, before I liked him.

When he turned to dip his pen in our inkwell, I was able to study his profile with its high-bridged nose, thick, close-knit eyebrows and cold grey eyes.

He always turned slowly, as a warrior in the saddle turns to observe any lagging members of his troop. Sometimes he would grant me an understanding smile, as though he had felt my gaze and wanted me to know that he appreciated my devotion and yet would prefer me to exercise a little moderation, a little restraint in admiring the back of his head, particularly as he had other merits besides his massive cranium.

In his movements in general I felt a solidity not usually found in thirteen- or fourteen-year-olds. But it was not the fake solidity affected by the swots and the beginners of the bootlicking tribe. It was the real thing that was to be found only in grown-up people.

True solidity, I would say, is the feeling of distinction a man acquires from being aware of a certain overabundance of physical weight in his every movement.

Now, if such a person enters a room and, let us say, sits down at your festive table and, having seated himself, casually motions the suddenly agitated guests to be seated as well, what, dear comrades, is the characteristic feature of this situation?

Its characteristic feature is that this superabundance of physical weight imparts to his gesture such gravity that he restores your guests to their places almost without looking at them at all, from which it follows that they were quite right to have become agitated on realising how morally lightweight and insecure they were in face of this extra weighty but indubitably pacific gesture.

So, during the movement of this hand which, though not too sweeping, is, happily, sufficiently prolonged, those at table who for one reason or another were not alerted in time manage to rouse themselves and now with a certain belated jubilation (like everything belated, exaggerated) jump to their feet and join in the general agitation so that they can subside with everyone else in obedience to the movement of the hand, which seems to say, "It's quite all right, comrades, I'll just squeeze into a corner somewhere..."

"What a man!" the assembled guests intimate with a delighted murmur and, having murmured, relax into a state of exhausted happiness.

That is what true solidity is!

And he, my idol, possessed such true solidity, that is to say, he was constantly aware of this extra physical weight in every movement. Admittedly, this weight was the direct result of a muscle development far beyond his years and not an expression of the burdens of authority, as in adults.

Yes, my idol was stronger than anyone not only in our class, but in what for us at that age was the whole conceivable world. And yet at first glance there was nothing special about him — just a stocky lad, by no means tall even for our class.

"That's for smoking, I don't grow because I smoke," he would say in the break, pulling at the home-made cigarette concealed in his fist, and it sounded rather as if this was divine punishment for his self-indulgence, although since the punishment atoned for the sin he was still able to speak of it calmly and go on smoking.

We lived in the same street. His name was Yura Stavrakidi and he was the youngest son in the large family of a house painter. He was always helping his father, particularly in summer. The painter's eldest son was by that time in the process of becoming an intellectual. Already a full-grown lad, he was in his last year at an industrial technical school, wore a neck-tie and could talk for hours about international politics. Yura and his father, one might say, were helping him to hold on to his intellectual laurels. But even he would now and then discard the neck-tie, change his clothes, take a paint brush and go off to work with his father and brother.

When they returned from work in the evening he would spend a long time washing in the yard. Yura would pour the water for him and, as I would be waiting for Yura, I had to put up with this lengthy procedure, which was not so easy.

It was the usual thing at this time for all those who liked discussing international events to gather in a corner of the yard.

Yura's brother, instead of getting on with washing himself, having his supper and going out to sit with them — if he couldn't do without this thing of his — would start bandying all kinds of ideas back and forth while washing, which endlessly prolonged the business and made me wild with impatience. Apparently in the course of the day's work he had grown hungry for this kind of talk because it certainly did not go down with his father, whose constant contact with bare walls during his long life as a painter had almost deprived him of the ability to converse.

All his life he had been busy silently daubing paint on walls and presumably had produced his children in the same silent fashion. And the more children he produced, the more walls he had to paint, so there had been no time left for talking; he had to get on with mixing his paints and obtaining enough whitewash. What was there to talk about anyhow! I think if he could have had his way he would have taken all those ranting and raving politicians and puttied up their mouths, ears and eyes, painted them from head to foot and left them standing deaf, dumb and blind, like those plaster statues we have in our parks. Or he might even have walled them up somewhere, and he would certainly have painted that wall so well that if you scraped it for a lifetime you would never discover the place where they were hidden. Because no matter how many children you brought into the world there would never be enough for their filthy meat-grinder, and no matter how many walls you painted your work would all be wasted because one air-raid would knock down so many, paint and all, that thousands of builders working all the year round still would not be able to restore them.

All this was written on his toilworn, gloomy face, the face of an old workman, and it had taken a tremendous war with all its disasters and hardships for this thought to emerge so that it could be seen by all, to make it show through his gloominess, just as a great fresco shows through on a neglected monastery wall.

Unfortunately, neither we children, nor Yura's brother, nor any of the other devotees of international affairs had any notion of this at the time. Yura's brother would go without bread as long as you let him hold forth on the subject of collective security, the machinations of the Vatican or something of that kind.

It always seemed to me unfair that he should start holding forth about all this even before he had finished washing and changing.

Besides, while he was slapping water on his face he would sometimes fail to hear what other people were saying and, having got everything wrong, have to ask them all over again. Or else he would scoop up some water in his hands and, instead of splashing it on his face, suddenly stop half way and listen while the water trickled through his fingers without his noticing it, and then he would slap his cheeks with empty hands and look suspiciously at Yura as though Yura was to blame for what had happened and for gathering all these talkers round him.

Sometimes, with his face all soapy, he would open his eyes, and then get into a temper because he thought he was being misunderstood whereas, in fact, as I could see perfectly well, it was simply the soap stinging his eyes. Or perhaps he would be asked a question just when he had given himself a silent slap on the back of the head, indicating the spot where Yura was to pour next and, while Yura was pouring, the others would stand round like stuffed dummies, waiting for the brother to raise his dripping head and regale them with his answer.

He went on talking while towelling himself, and even while pulling on his shirt he never stopped asking questions and giving answers.

Sometimes it was simply ridiculous. Before he got his head out of the shirt he would start muttering away inside it, as though we could understand what he was muttering about. And sometimes he couldn't get his head out at all because he had forgotten to unbutton the collar. But would he unbutton it himself? Oh no, this darling of the family would wait like a baby to be unbuttoned by Yura and meanwhile go on jabbering in this strange head-in-a-tent attitude.

He was just like the mad photographer who came to take pictures of us at school. Having pulled his black hood over his head, he would start muttering remarks that we couldn't understand, or at least we pretended we couldn't because we felt we had a right not to. Who likes being talked at from under a hood anyway? In the end he would flap out from under its folds and, having recovered his breath, issue all kinds of instructions about who should sit where, then take another gulp of air and dive under the hood again.

Similarly Yura's brother would in the end — admittedly only with Yura's help — get his head through the shirt and go off to his friends, tucking his shirt-tails in as he went. That, thank goodness, he did himself.

But then Yura's mother would appear on the porch and call out in Greek that supper was ready and he would ignore her and so persistently that she would begin to scold him and shout at him to finish his "jabber-jabber conference".

Who knows, perhaps this expression was coined by her, but to this day that is what the people of our town call any long spell of talking. At one time this expression used to irritate me. It struck me as inaccurate and incomplete. Its meaning seemed to flop about in a much too large envelope of sound. But later I realised that this flopping about is indeed the highest form of accuracy, because even in the actual phenomena of life the concept an expression implies flops about just as uselessly. Luckily, as time went on, Yura's brother returned less and less frequently to his father's profession and I seldom had to suffer their joint washing operation while waiting for Yura.

I can still see the long shrivelled figure of Yura's

father, his face overgrown with whitewash-like stubble, and Yura beside him, stripped to the waist and spattered with whitewash, a long brush over his shoulder. In the light of the setting sun he looked as magnificent as a young Hercules walking home from work beside his old father.

When he had washed and eaten his supper, he would come out into the street, still stripped to the waist as before, and we would all sit together on the sun-warmed steps of the porch and Yura would tell us about the people he and his father had been working for that day. His hands would be lying limply on his knees, his face would be a little pale from fatigue, and I would relish the pleasure he himself and his every muscle felt from being still.

If he and his father had been working for a generous employer who knew how to feed his men well, Yura would go on about what dishes they had been given and how much he personally had eaten, and how he and his father had tried to do as good a job as possible just to please their employer.

In summer Yura often visited his Greek relatives in the country. On his return he would tell us what the life was like there, what they ate and how much.

"I carried a hundredweight sack all the way from Tsebelda in six hours," would be his next bit of information. That was his sports news.

"All the way from Tsebelda on foot?" a surprised voice would say. In such cases there would always be one voice expressing the general surprise.

"Of course," Yura would reply, and then add, "I did eat a loaf of bread and a kilo of butter on the road."

"How could you eat a kilo of butter, Yura?" the expresser of the general surprise would ask.

"It's country butter, Greek butter," Yura would explain. "You can eat it without bread if you like."

But besides his physical strength, what I would now call his games sense was amazingly well developed too, and showed itself in most unexpected ways.

There is no need to relate here the well-known case when he got on a bicycle for the first time and after a

94

push from someone and a couple of wobbles with the handle bars rode away quite calmly.

The same kind of thing once happened at sea. For some reason Yura hardly ever swam. Despite his incredible daring I believe he never trusted the water. He knew how to stay afloat and would swim out a little way in country style, but then turn back, find the bottom with his feet and walk ashore. Either it was because he had grown up in a mountain village and not on the coast, or because, like his ancient compatriot, he could do nothing without a good foothold, but it was very hard to tempt him out of his depth; he would swim out a mere five or six metres and then turn back to the shore.

As a person already much inclined to indulge in the simple forms of pleasure, I could stay in the water for hours and I was, of course, disappointed by his restrained attitude towards the sea. One day after much persuasion I got him to go with me to the swimming pool. We undressed and went up on to the board over the fifty-metre lanes. Among the foppish, though almost naked, denizens of the pool he looked decidedly out of place in a pair of shorts that came down to his knees.

He tried to climb down into the water, but I persuaded him to dive. We decided to swim along together so that I could study his movements, get him used to swimming out of his depth and in the end teach him something like a proper modern style.

Yura jumped into the water — feet first, of course. I shall never forget the expression of confusion combined with a readiness to resist that was written on his face when he came up. It was the kind of expression a hunted man might have when leaping out of bed in the middle of the night and grabbing his gun.

However, having convinced himself that no one was going to pull him under, he swam off to the opposite end. He swam his usual stern overarm stroke, turning his head after every thrust, as though guarding his rear.

After waiting a few seconds I dived in after him. I had to tell him not to turn his head like that.

I had decided to go straight into the crawl after my dive and overtake him all in one breath, so to speak, without coming up for air.

When I did raise my head out of the water I looked at the lane beside me, but Yura was not there. He was still in front. The distance between us had scarcely lessened. He was still turning his head at every stroke and making good progress.

Working hard with my legs, I switched to the breast stroke but, try as I would, the gap between us remained the same. I was baffled. His head went on turning at every sweep of his arm and his eyes gave a grim stare now over the right shoulder, now over the left.

When I finally reached him he was already resting, or rather waiting for me, holding on to the bars at the other end of the pool.

"Well, how did I swim?" he asked.

I looked into his grey eyes but found no mockery there.

"Pretty good, but don't keep turning your head," I replied, trying not to show my heavy breathing, and also clutched the bars for support.

In answer to this he rubbed his neck a little and silently swam away to the other end. I watched him. The funny way he had of turning his head to right and left and throwing his arm out too straight diverted attention from the powerful underwater work of his arms and legs.

He swam like a powerful animal in a strange but manageable environment. That straight neck and indomitable head jutted proudly out of the water. I realised that I should never catch up with him on land or sea.

I think my liking for the simple forms of pleasure helped me to overcome a mean-spirited envy. Anyway, I decided, his victory at sea only proved once again how right I was in my choice of an object of worship.

Not far from our street there was a large and ancient park. In recent times some sports facilities had been set up there, including a huge cross-beam on posts to which was fixed a whole system of gymnastic equipment: a pole, rings, ropes and a set of wall-bars. Naturally Yura was way ahead of us all on every piece of this equipment.

But he, my idol, was not only strong and agile, he was also the boldest of us all, and this caused me a vague feeling of anxiety.

He would climb up the wall-bars on to the cross-beam itself, sit astride it for a while, then let go with his hands and carefully stand up. And then came the miracle of daring.

As we watched with bated breath he would sway gently until the cross-beam was swaying with him. The posts that held it had been weakened by the constant pull of the rope, which was used as a swing, so the whole structure was soon in motion.

When he had got it moving like this, he would suddenly, with well timed steps run quickly along the beam from one end to the other. In the few seconds it took him to reach the other end the beam would sway so violently that it looked as if he would lose his balance and fall right off. But he made it every time.

The top of the cross-beam was no wider than a man's hand and there were bolts sticking out of it, so in addition to everything else he had to be careful not to trip over them as he ran.

We all breathed with relief when he finally lowered his hands to the beam and climbed down by way of the wall-bars. This star turn by my idol never failed to astound the spectators and he always performed it with maximum risk — always swaying the beam first and always running, never walking.

I don't know why, but I conceived a desperate desire to try myself out at this high-altitude trick. I chose a time when none of our crowd were in the park and climbed the wall-bars. While I still had a foothold on them, the beam did not seem so terribly high. But as soon as my feet were on the beam itself, I felt very high-up and unprotected.

I squatted on my haunches, gripping the beam with both hands, and tried to gauge the quiet oscillation of the whole system. It was like being on the back of a sleeping animal. I could feel its breathing and was afraid of waking it.

At last I let go and straightened up. Trying not to

97

look down, I took one step and without lifting my other foot from the beam dragged it up to the first. The whole structure was swaying gently under me. Ahead lay a narrow green path studded with protruding bolts that I should have to be careful of as well.

I took another step forward and cautiously drew up the other foot, but not quite cautiously enough apparently, because the structure came to life and heaved under me. Trying to keep my balance, I froze to the spot and looked down.

The ground, red with fallen pine needles and reinforced with exposed roots, swam beneath me.

"Go back before it's too late," I told myself and gingerly turned my head. The end of the beam I had just left was quite close, but I realised at once that I should not be able to turn round. Turning round on such a narrow ledge would be worse than going forward.

I felt trapped. Either I must sit down astride the beam and ease myself backwards, or I must continue on my way. Frightened though I was, some inner force prevented me from making so shameful a retreat. I went forward. Sometimes, as I began to lose my balance, I thought I had better jump rather than fall off but somehow I managed to steady myself and go on. I walked right to the other end and, now afraid that sheer joy might topple me, bent down and put my arms right round the beam, hugging it and appreciating its no longer dangerous swaying. It goes without saying that I did not keep my little exploit a secret from the others. Yura himself looked hard at me, then offered his congratulations. I repeated the trick several times afterwards, but my fear grew hardly any less; it was simply that I got used to the idea of mastering a fear of a certain intensity and mastered it.

It seems to me that in any kind of action the initial fear is so powerful because it comes as a sensation of stepping into a yawning abyss, into endless horror. When we overcome this fear, we do not remove the sense of danger, but find a measure for that which we used to regard as infinite. The man who finds a measure for non-being will provide us all with the best antidote for the fear of death.

Some of the others also learned to walk the swaying beam, but neither they nor I ever tried to run along it. We sensed that this was only for the chosen few, and only in our secret dreams did we ever repeat his exploit.

...In the vision of Christ walking across the water there is something of the charlatanism of the Grand Inquisitor. What we see is people being lured into religion by means of a miracle. But the operation would have been equally successful if Christ had turned the pebbles on the shore into gold coins before the eyes of those fishermen.

There was nothing spiritual in his walking the waters because he had nothing to overcome. He could walk on water because he was incorporeal or because he was held up with an invisible thread by the Chief Designer. So all he had to do was walk the waters in a Worthy Way, with the kind of modest dignity with which those elected to the presidium mount the platform at meetings.

Our Yura was quite a different case. There he stands on that cross-beam. He is preparing himself for an heroic exploit, for a man-made miracle. His whole figure, the aggressive thrust of his body, the bunching of his limbs as if for a spring, the concentration in his face, all express the fierce contest between courage and fear. He takes off and for a few seconds of Olympian victory spirit conquers flesh!

Before our eyes he drove his body from one end of the beam to the other like an audacious rider forcing his unwilling steed across a foaming mountain torrent. It was beautiful and we all felt it, although none of us could have explained why, at the time.

One day Yura suggested to me that we should rob the school cafeteria, and although we had never done anything of the kind before, I agreed without a second thought. Neither of us felt any pangs of conscience because this was not our school and because it was also very convenient for burglary, being next door to our house. The temptation arose from the sausages that, according to reliable rumours, had been brought to the cafeteria that day.

The plan was simple. We were to break in, eat all the sausages, take all the change out of the cash-desk and make our getaway. We were not going to steal any paper money because we knew that it was never left in the till. Curiously enough, we never considered taking any of the sausages with us; we simply couldn't imagine that there might be too many. This was not because in an operation run by my idol with his Tsebelda experience there was no need to worry on that score, but because our general experience told us that no one anywhere ever left sausages uneaten. Neither of us had ever heard of such a thing.

In the afternoon we strolled into the cafeteria to spy out the lie of the land.

A large bowl festooned with sausages was standing on the windowsill. It was bathed in a pink radiance from the slanting rays of the evening sun.

Yura stared at this apparition with such sentimental candour that in the end I had to steer him away because his curiosity was beginning to look indecent and dangerous.

"It's too much for me," he said, taking a deep breath when we stopped in the corridor by the window.

"What's too much?" I asked quietly.

"When they're burst like that," he replied drawing breath with a whistling sound, as if he had taken a sausage that was too hot for him.

I felt my mouth watering too.

"Wait till this evening," I whispered, appealing for fortitude.

We left the building.

The best way of entering the school at night was through the permanently locked back-door. The door had glass panels, but one of them was broken and the opening was wide enough to climb through.

There was a store-keeper who lived on the premises and in addition to his other duties performed that of watchman. We had been at war with him for many years because we liked to use the school yard for football and he tried to keep us out.

He was, unfortunately, a hale and hearty old man. As soon as it grew properly dark we climbed into the school yard and crept over to the locked door. It showed up faintly in the dim light from the street and the black

100

hole left by the missing pane looked menacing. From the street came the voices of our lads. They sounded remote, like distant echoes of a peaceful life that we had left irrevocably behind us. A large puddle glistened oilily just in front of the door. I stepped round it carefully and looked in through the hole.

"In you go," said Yura, and I climbed in.

With one hand I found a hold on the wall and with the other gripped the door handle, pulled my legs up and pushed them through the hole, trying to feel the floor inside with my feet. In this position of moral and physical suspense I dangled for a time, wiggling my toes and slipping gradually until I felt the floor and was able to pull the upper part of my body inside.

Overhanging the corridor was the first flight of the stairs leading to the attic. We had to go along the corridor, then turn down another corridor at the end of which was the cafeteria.

Yura climbed in quickly after me and we advanced along the corridor, stopping every now and then and listening to the eerie silence of the locked classrooms and the dark deserted school.

My heart beat so hard that with every step I had to overcome its recoil. When we passed a window my friend's stern profile would appear in the darkness and I would feel less frightened. I have forgotten to say that for some reason I was wearing a white shirt. More suitable for a ghost than a burglar, it loomed a ghastly white in the darkness, as though I were dressed in my own fear. I tried not to look at it to keep my anxiety at bay.

We reached the door of the cafeteria. A faint ray of light shone through the crack. Yura pressed on the door; the crack widened and he put his eye to it.

He kept his eye to that crack for a long time, as though trying to get a glimpse of the night life of the sausages or the other inhabitants of the cafeteria. Finally he turned a more cheerful face towards me and signalled me to look through the crack as well, as if offering me a portion of good cheer before engaging in the most dangerous part of our enterprise. I peeped in and again saw our sausages. They were still in the same place, but now, covered with a piece of cheesecloth, they looked even more tempting.

Yura took a pair of pincers that we had obtained beforehand and set to work on the padlock. It was a matter of pulling out one of the rings to which the lock was attached. But this was not so easy.

Excited by the sight of the sausages, he began to hurry and the pincers slipped off the ring several times with a rather loud clank.

And suddenly I heard quite distinctly the sound of footsteps on the floor above us. Whoever it was walked on for a few more steps, and then stopped, as if listening.

"Let's run for it!" I whispered in panic, but at once felt his fingers gripping my forearm.

We stood stiff and silent in the long stillness of the corridor.

"You imagined it," Yura whispered at last.

I shook my head. We stiffened again.

I don't know how long we stood like this. In the end Yura turned back to the door, as though comparing the degree of risk with the degree of temptation. He listened again, peeped through the crack, listened, and then set about the lock in real earnest.

And suddenly those footsteps came again! Once more Yura's hand, forestalling my reflex of desertion, gripped my arm.

But the footsteps did not stop. Now they were clearly approaching down the stairs. They hesitated for a moment and suddenly a beam of light, reaching us sooner than the click of the switch, descended from the upper floor like the blast of an explosion and the footsteps started again.

Yura's hand relaxed its grip on my arm. The wild and unerring horse of fear carried me off and threw me out of the school building. I didn't stop for a second at the hole in the door. I shot straight through it and opened my eyes when I landed in the puddle. Only when I had scrambled over the fence did I notice that Yura was not with me. I did not know what to think. Surely the watchman hadn't caught him? If he had, why hadn't I heard anything?

I observed the school through the fence, waiting for a flashing of lights and buzzing of angry little alarm bells, and then for the militia to arrive...

But time passed and all was quiet and I began to notice how dirty my white shirt was. I should be in trouble for that at home and would have to slip in quietly, throw the shirt in with the dirty linen and put on something else.

Lost in these depressing thoughts, I noticed Yura only when he swung himself over the fence and landed beside me.

What had happened? Apparently, when we were running away from the watchman, he had sensed that we should not be able to get out of the building together and had had the presence of mind to run up the attic staircase and wait there for the danger to pass. And he had thought of that in the few seconds while we were running away!

I could never have thought of such a thing so quickly. I had darted like an animal back through the hole I had come in by, but Yura... Well, that was what he was like, my old friend Yura Stavrakidi.

Reading over what I have written I recalled that according to the best literary formulas one should also say a few words about shortcomings of one's hero. They were, of course, insignificant and did nothing to darken his shining aspect; they merely shaded it in a little. The existence of such defects — only small ones, I must repeat — should bring him nearer to us, make him more human and even, perhaps, evoke an understanding smile. People are only human, after all.

I must admit that Yura liked a fight. In those days we all liked fighting, but Yura for quite natural reasons was particularly fond of this pastime.

He would fight to defend his own honour, or Greek honour, or simply that of the weak and defenceless, or the honour of painters, quite often the honour of our street and, less often, that of our class. And sometimes he would fight for no particular reason, when the two sides merely wanted to measure their strength so that they could afterwards jump to a higher branch of the genealogical tree of chivalry, or yield their own branch, as the case might be.

103

"I want to fight him," Yura would say to me quietly, nodding at some boy or other. Usually this was a newcomer who had only just appeared at our school or in the neighbourhood of our street. Or sometimes this was one of our old acquaintances who had suddenly grown much bigger or filled out during the summer and now required — though he might not wish it himself — a reassessment of his potential.

So Yura would nod in his direction and there was such ardour and secret happiness in his face that I could not help admiring him. Such probably is the admiration of the gardener who finds a prematurely ripened fruit in his orchard and carefully bends the branch to examine it, or perhaps of a Don Juan viewing from afar a new beloved with a similar significant tenderness.

Usually the boy would sooner or later become aware of Yura's secret passion and a shy embarrassment would appear in his movements that would eventually break out into arrogance.

"He feels it too," Yura would say, nodding joyfully in his direction and his eyes would glow with the goat-like cunning of a little satyr.

One day Yura and I were standing at the entrance to what was at the time I am writing of our best cinema, the *Apsny*. There was some fabulous film on and the street around us was surging with youngsters. Many were looking for tickets and would peer into our eyes, trying to spot someone who had bought a ticket for the purpose of reselling it.

How pleasant it was to be able to stand in the crowd before the show began and feel the ticket in your pocket, knowing there were so many yearning to get one but you had yours so you had nothing to fear. And when the doors opened you would also be able to stroll round the foyer, inspecting for the hundredth time the delightful daubs of a local artist on themes from Pushkin's fairy-tales, relishing the knowledge that these little pleasures were all for free and the main pleasure was yet to come. And after that, when they let you into the hall, which

would be positively steaming from the previous show
and redolent of the pleasure that had just been experienced
by others and was still in store for you, there would be the
newsreel, a feeble one perhaps but also in the nature
of a free gift with the real pleasure yet to come, and
perhaps the sweetest thing in life was to keep putting it off
and putting it off since happiness, once begun, could not be
stretched for ever, because it might break, like the film
itself.

And this was the state of blissful suspense in which
I was standing when a boy came up to Yura.

"Got a ticket?"

Yura looked at the lad, such a puny, such a ticketless
little fellow, and paused as if to let him feel the full
depth of his nothingness, and said, "Yes, I have, but I'm
going myself."

"I see you're trying to be funny," the boy retorted
cheekily, emboldened by disappointment.

"Yes, I was," Yura agreed. He seemed unable to believe
his ears, unable to comprehend that from this depth of
nothingness anyone could possibly answer him back, and
was now testing his own senses to see if he had not perhaps
imagined this impudent voice.

"But it didn't come off, did it?" the boy said and with
a vengeful nod turned to go away.

"Wait a minute," Yura started forward.

The boy halted fearlessly.

"So I'm a speculator, am I?" Yura asked unexpectedly
and, seizing him by the lapels of his jacket, shook him.
"I'm a speculator, am I?" he repeated.

I felt a sour taste in my mouth. This was my body's
as yet unconscious reaction to what was dishonourable
and unfair.

I sensed that Yura wanted to fight the boy, but that
would have been beyond all borings. The boy obviously did
not want to fight, he was obviously the weaker of the two,
he had not said that Yura was a speculator, and he wasn't
even a gingerhead.

"So I'm a speculator, am I?" Yura repeated, and
tried to shake him into fighting form.

"I didn't say that," the boy's voice began to quaver,

and he looked round in search of friends or protectors.

"Yes, you did!" Yura shook him again, striving to elicit some further insult, so that he could let fly. But the boy would not be provoked and this annoyed Yura even more because he might have to take final step himself. And it looked as if he was going to.

But at that moment half a dozen Greek boys appeared from nowhere and surrounded us, chanting in one voice, "Aren't you ashamed, Greek? ... *Kendrepeso...*" came the familiar words out of the din.

Apparently they knew both Yura and the other boy well and Yura for some reason had to reckon with them. And this boy, so obviously Russian in appearance, suddenly, as if from sheer fright, also began to babble in Greek so fluently that even Yura was confused. Apparently the boy lived in the same yard as these lads.

They went on like this for some time, raising and lowering their voices, going over from Russian to Greek and back to Russian. Yura maintained that although the boy had not actually called him a speculator, he had asked how much he would sell his ticket for, which obviously meant ... and so on.

"I didn't say that. It's not true," the boy argued, boldly now that he was surrounded by his Greek friends.

"Aren't you ashamed, Greek?" again the Greeks appealed to Yura's conscience in their own language.

"Ask him, if you don't believe me," Yura said, and turned towards me.

I had been expecting this. I hated him at that moment. I would have liked to tread on his handsome, lying face, but he was my friend and by some ancient law of comradeship, fellow-countrymanship, kinship or whatever, I was bound to defend him, while another, stronger but for some reason illegitimate feeling prompted me to take the side of the other boy.

Everyone looked at me, confident that I would take Yura's side, if only because he had appealed to me. But for the first second I hesitated and by so doing at once roused intense curiosity, because if I was his friend and had not leapt to his defence I must be going to say something unusual or perhaps even tell the whole truth.

They all stared at me in hushed expectation and I felt that every moment of my silence was lifting me to intrepid heights in their eyes. Indeed, I myself felt how high I was rising in my silence, how fruitful it was in itself, and yet at the same time, knowing in advance that I should fail them as soon as I opened my mouth, I waited for the moment when it would be simply too dangerous to go any higher in view of the inevitable subsequent fall.

"I didn't hear," I said, and acid spurted into my mouth as if I had bitten into the crabbiest of all crab apples.

Both sides instantly lost interest in me and returned to their argument, now relying only on their own forces. The bell rang.

We sat together watching the film. Sometimes from the corner of my eye I caught a glimpse of my friend's stern face that was becoming more and more estranged.

On the way home I tried to explain something, but he was unresponsive.

"Let's not start a jabber-jabber conference," he said as we reached his house and he turned into the court-yard.

That was the beginning of the end of our friendship. We did not quarrel. We simply lost our common aim. Gradually we left the childhood we had shared and entered a youth that we could not share because youth was the beginning of specialisation of the soul. And in purely physical terms, through circumstances beyond our control we lost touch with each other.

It was only many years later that we met again in our town on the upper floor of the off-shore restaurant *Amra*. I had dropped in for a cup of coffee. He was sitting with a group of local lads. We recognised each other from a distance and he rose, smiling broadly, from his table.

I sat down with him and, as custom required, we re-called our schooldays and old friends.

Yura was now a naval officer, serving somewhere up north. He was on a long leave. He had come here for a holiday and a good time and was then going to spend the rest of his leave in Kazakhstan, where his parents were now living.

I reminded him of his running along the beam and confessed that this feat of his had remained for me a great and never-to-be-fulfilled ambition.

"I could never have walked it," Yura said, with a shrug.

"Couldn't you?"

"I was far too scared to take it slowly," he said, and a ghost of the old fearlessness appeared in his eye for a moment.

"You don't mean it!" I exclaimed, feeling that his confession imposed some sort of obligation on me, though I did not know yet what it was.

"Do you know why I used to make it sway?" he asked and, without waiting for my answer, replied, "I thought a steady rolling would be better than sudden plunges... Like at sea," he added, consoling me with a more universal application of his discovery.

No, I had no regrets about my adolescent enthusiasm for his feat. I merely felt that courage, like cowardice, too, probably, was of a more complex nature than I had previously suspected, and much of what I had once believed to be clearly solved after all had probably not been solved so exactly.

It made me sad. Scraps of half-formed thoughts prevented me from enjoying myself, as exams still waiting to be taken had done when I was a student.

I wanted to go home at once and form a final opinion at least about something. But I had to stay because the waitress arrived with what had been ordered. She had brought a bottle of brandy and a skilfully cut water melon, which as soon as the plate was on the table opened out trickling with juice, like a huge lotus with flaming red petals.

Yura's hand went out to the bottle. No, of course, I couldn't leave.

OLD CROOKED ARM

I have told the story of how in my childhood, when finding my way at night to the house of a relative of ours, I fell into a freshly dug grave, where I spent several hours in the company of a stray goat, until I and the goat were rescued by a passing peasant. That was during the war.

Some time after this nocturnal adventure, we, that is, my mother, sister and I, went to live in that very village. At first, we stayed with my mother's sister, then we found a room in another house and moved.

The house had been occupied before the war by three brothers. They were all in the army. One of them had married before enlisting and now his young, blooming and not too grief-stricken wife was all alone in the house. Remembering her now, I am drawn to the conclusion that a grass widow is called a grass widow because she catches fire as easily as dry grass.

While we were living there, one of the brothers came home. Yes, the one that was married. He came home a little too quietly somehow. We noticed him in the kitchen one morning. He was sitting in front of the fire roasting a corncob on a spit, as though to remind himself of his pre-war childhood. There was something about him that made one think he ought not to have come home just yet. Or perhaps, he ought not to have married quite so soon, because I think it was missing his wife so badly that brought him home too early.

He pottered about in the garden with a kind of desperate eagerness for a week or so, then he was arrested; and shortly afterwards we heard that he was a deserter. He was arrested just as quietly as he had arrived.

We gradually settled down in the new place. My

sister obtained work at the local collective farm as a time-keeper; we were allotted a patch of land, on which we grew melons and maize. We also grew pumpkins on it, and cucumbers and tomatoes, too. In those days we used to grow everything.

Well, it so happened that not far from our house there lived the very man whose grave I had fallen into. Incidentally, people in the village used to say that everyone had fallen into that grave except the man it was meant for. The story turned out to be long and complex. The grave's future owner, if one may so describe him, old Shchaaban Larba, nicknamed Crooked Arm, had been in hospital with either appendicitis or rupture. (In Russian, it would probably be more correct to call him Withered Arm, but Crooked Arm corresponds more closely to the spirit and, hence, the meaning of the nickname.) Well, as I was saying, Crooked Arm had had an operation, and he was still in hospital, calmly recovering his health, when someone telephoned from the hospital to our village Soviet to say that the patient had died and would have to be collected and taken home immediately because he had been lying dead for more than a day already.

None of the sick man's relatives had been visiting the hospital just then because he had been about to be discharged.

True, a fellow villager, Mustafa, had been in town at the time on business of his own and had, incidentally, been asked to call at the hospital and find out why Crooked Arm was still there, and whether he had not perhaps decided to have his crooked arm put right as well as the appendicitis or rupture. And then, all of a sudden, such unexpected news.

The dead man's relatives, as our customs demand, sent out messengers of woe to the neighbouring villages, a large army cape was stretched across the yard of his house to make a shelter where the funeral feast would be held, and a grave was dug in the cemetery.

The collective farm sent its one and only lorry to bring the dead man home because private transport was hard to come by in wartime. In short, the whole thing was arranged in proper style, just as it should be. Yes, everything was as it should be, except the dead man himself, Shchaaban Larba, who, so it was said, had never given anyone any peace while he was alive, and after death became quite unmanageable.

The day after the sorrowful news the lorry arrived back in the village with the body of the dead man, who turned out to be alive.

Crooked Arm, they say, walked into the yard of his house gently supported by Mustafa and swearing loudly. His indignation was due not to the news of his death and the preparations for his funeral but to something he noticed at once on glancing at the shelter made with the army cape, for which two apple trees had been stripped of their branches. Still swearing, Crooked Arm demonstrated on the spot how the cape could have been hung without touching the trees.

After that, they say, he made the round of his guests, shaking hands with each and staring keenly into their eyes to discover what impression had been caused by the news of his death and simultaneous, quite unexpected, resurrection.

Having done this, they say, he raised that arm of his, which had been withering for twenty years but still had not withered away, and, shading his eyes with his hand, peered rudely at the women who had been hired to weep for him, as though he didn't know what they were there for.

"What do *you* want?" he rasped.

They looked embarrassed. "Oh, nothing special. We just came to weep for you."

"Well, get on with it then," Crooked Arm is said to have replied, and put his hand to his ear to listen to the weeping. But at this point someone intervened and led the weepers away.

When he saw the gifts that his relatives had brought, Crooked Arm pondered for a moment. It is the custom among my people to hold any kind of funeral feast on such a grand scale that, were it all done at the expense of the dead man's family, its surviving members would have no alternative but to lie down and die as well.

So, all the relatives and neighbours help out. Some bring wine, some bring roast chickens, some bring *khacha-*

puri, and someone may even bring a calf. And it so happened this time that one of the relatives from the next village had brought along a well fattened calf, which Crooked Arm took an immediate liking to. Incidentally, they say that it was from this relative that the measurements had been taken for digging the grave, because he was just about the same height as Crooked Arm. They say that when one of the lads who had been told to dig the grave came up to him with a measuring string, this relative expressed some displeasure and argued that there were other people more suitable for the purpose, that he was probably a little taller than Crooked Arm and Crooked Arm was more stocky.

So saying, he tried to get away from the measuring string, but the lad would not let him get away. Like all grave-diggers, this lad was given to joking. He said that Crooked Arm's stockiness made no difference now, and that if the worst came to the worst and Crooked Arm was not the right size, they would have his relative in mind.

The relative, they say, sniggered half-heartedly at these jokes, but evidently took offence, because he withdrew to the company of the people from his own village and stood with them, glancing sulkily at his calf, which was tethered to the fence.

At the sight of all these gifts Crooked Arm announced that it was too early yet to rejoice, that he still felt very ill, and that he had been discharged only so that he should not die in hospital because doctors were fined for that, just as collective farmers were fined for spoiled produce. He then went straight to bed and gave instructions that the grave should on no account be filled in, but kept open in readiness. The relatives, it is said, dispersed somewhat unwillingly, the one who had brought the calf being particularly displeased. But Crooked Arm calmed him with assurances that he would not have long to wait, so the calf would not waste away even if it was not let out of the yard.

Crooked Arm stayed in bed for about a week. After a couple of days he began to be pestered by the curious, because by that time the rumour had spread that Crooked Arm, having died in the hospital, had come to life on the way home and arrived there for his own funeral. Another

112

rumour had it that he had not died at all but had fallen into a deep sleep from which the doctors had been unable to awake him, but the journey back had been so bumpy that he had woken up of his own accord.

At first Crooked Arm received the visitors, particularly while they continued to bring him all kinds of delicacies designed to tempt the palate of a man who had recently been dead and was still not quite alive again. But eventually he grew tired of this, and in any case the chairman of the farm said there was work to be done. So, when he heard the gate creak, he would run out on the veranda and bellow in his loud voice, "Back! Keep back, you parasites! I'll set the dog on you!"

However, the rumours of his resurrection grew and multiplied. It must have been quite a year later when I heard in one of the neighbouring villages that Crooked Arm had come to life not on the way home from hospital, but actually in his grave, several days after burial. The noise he had been making was heard by a boy who had been looking for his goat one evening in the cemetery. So the villagers had to go and dig him out. If he had not possessed such a powerful voice, they said, he would have died of hunger, or even of thirst, because the site that had been chosen for his grave was a good one — well drained.

So it came about that Crooked Arm survived or, at least, prevented his own funeral, while retaining for himself a grave in complete readiness.

When they first saw Crooked Arm on his return from hospital, the people of the village decided that it was the secretary of the village Soviet who had played a joke on them, because he was the man who had said he had talked with the hospital or someone who had pretended to be the hospital. But the secretary declared that he would never dream of playing such a joke with a war on.

Everyone believed him, because to joke like that in war-time would have been just a bit too stupid. Eventually, it was agreed that there had been some sort of mix-up at the hospital, that another old man had died, perhaps even one of Crooked Arm's namesakes, for in Abkhazia we have any number of people of the very same name.

I heard Crooked Arm's voice the first day we started

113

living with our grass widow, even before I had met him face to face. At exactly midday, when he was coming home for dinner from work on the farm, he would at a distance of some three hundred metres from his house start shouting to his wife, scolding her and inquiring furiously if the hominy was ready.

The old woman would respond with equally frantic yells and their voices with no loss of power or clarity would gradually come together, overreach each other and at last fall silent. After a time the old woman's voice would shoot up triumphantly from the silence but Crooked Arm's would not respond. Later on, when I began visiting their house, I realised that the old man kept quiet at this stage for the simple reason that his mouth was occupied with eating; he ate as frantically as he cursed, so he could not possibly eat and curse at the same time.

Coming home from work in the evening, he would inquire in the same tone of voice about his horse or his grandson Yashka and again about the hominy for supper.

Later on, I made friends with this Yashka, who was just as loud-voiced as his grandfather but, unlike him, a good-natured lounger. Crooked Arm usually took him to school on the back of his horse, and would curse all the way there over having to waste his precious time on this dunderhead. Yashka would sit in silence behind his grandfather, holding on to his belt and gazing around with a sheepish grin on his face.

If his grandfather was away, he would be taken to school by his grandmother on the same horse, and he would sit behind her in the same way, except that he did not let her ride right up to the school in case the boys made fun of him.

He and I attended school in different shifts. On my way home from school I would meet them about halfway and Yashka would screw his head round and stare wistfully after me, thereby touching off a fresh explosion of fury from his grandfather. Yashka had to be taken to school because it was three kilometres from his home and Yashka was so absentminded that he sometimes forgot where he was going and took the wrong road.

In the early days, on meeting me in the street, Crooked

Arm would look at me shading his eyes with his hand, and ask:

"Who do you belong to?"

"I am the son of so-and-so," I would answer politely and give the name of my mother, whom he had known for many years.

"Who's she?" he would thunder, and scrutinise me even more thoroughly from under his crooked palm.

"She is Uncle Meksut's wife's sister," I would explain, though I realised he was pretending.

"So you're one of those parasites from town?" he would say with a nod in the direction of our house.

"Yes," I would reply, confirming that we lived there and at the same time reluctantly acknowledging our role as parasites.

He would stand before me, peering at me in astonishment with his gimlet eyes, a rather short, stocky man with a massive neck as red as a cock's comb. And while he stood there, peering at me in surprise, as though to achieve a complete mental picture of me, he would at the same time be listening to something else, to something that was taking place on the other side of the fence, in the maize on his allotment, as though he could tell by whispers, by scuffling, by sounds audible to his ears alone exactly what was happening on his allotment, in his yard and perhaps even inside the house itself.

"So it was you who fell into my grave?" he would ask suddenly, listening as usual to what was happening on his allotment and already sensing something amiss that made him snort with dissatisfaction.

"Yes," I would reply, observing him with secret misgiving, because I felt he was packed with some kind of explosive force.

"And what did you think of it down there?" he would ask, still with one ear to the fence, as it were, and becoming more and more agitated over what was happening on the other side of it, and even beginning to mutter to himself, "Is that old woman dead, or what? Curse her eyes... She'll ruin me one of these days, the old fool..."

"Very nice," I would reply, trying to display my gratitude for the hospitality. After all, it was his grave.

115

"It's a good, dry spot," he would agree, almost whining with indignation at what was happening on his allotment; and all of a sudden he would let fly and shout to his old woman, leaping straight to his top note: "Hey! There's something grunting in the kitchen garden! Blast your ears — it's the pigs, the pigs!"

"May I bury them with you in that grave of yours! You see pigs everywhere!" the old woman would retort at once.

"But I can hear them — they're munching and grunting, munching and grunting!" he would shout, forgetting all about me, and, as usual, their voices overlapped and he seemed to snatch the end of her shout and haul himself along by it towards the house, tossing her his own raging voice as he went. By and by we grew accustomed to his voice and stopped paying much attention to it, and when he was away for a few days and all was quiet and still, it seemed strange, as though something was missing and our ears were full of an empty roar.

His wife, a tall old woman, taller than he, and unbelievably thin, would sometimes, when he was not at home, come round for a chat with my mother. She would occasionally bring a cheese or a bowl of maize flour or a fragrant lump of meat that had been smoked over an outdoor fire. With a shy little laugh she would ask us to hide away what she had brought and, for goodness sake, never say thank you, because that bawling husband of hers must not know anything about it.

She and my mother would talk for hours and Crooked Arm's wife would smoke all the time, making herself cigarette after cigarette. Suddenly Crooked Arm's voice would be heard. He would shout something to her in the direction of their house and she would prick up her ears at the sound of his voice and shake with silent laughter, as though she were afraid he would hear her laughing at him for shouting in the wrong direction.

"What do you want now — I'm over here!" she would shout in the end.

"Aha, idling again! Birds of a feather! You're nothing but a gang of chatterboxes!" he would bawl, after a brief pause during which he must have been struck dumb with indignation at her treachery.

One day he rode up to our gate and shouted to me to bring out a sack. Grumbling loudly about parasites who had to have everything chewed and put in their mouths for them to swallow, he filled my sack half full of flour and, still fuming because he was giving away his own maize that he had had to take to the mill on his own horse, he tied his sack to the saddle again and rode away, bawling over his shoulder that I must be careful not to tell that woman anything about the flour because he never had any peace from her shrieking as it was.

Time went by and Old Crooked Arm showed no signs of dying. The longer he delayed his death, the more the calf flourished and grew fat; the more the calf flourished and grew fat, the sadder its former owner became. In the end he sent a man to Crooked Arm to drop a hint about the calf. Thank the Lord Crooked Arm was still alive, the message ran, but now it would be only right to return the calf, because he had not made Crooked Arm a present of it; he had only brought it to the funeral as a good kinsman should.

"Brought an egg and wants to go home with a chicken," Crooked Arm is said to have responded. After this, they say, he thought for a moment and added: "Tell him that if I die soon he can come to the funeral without any offering at all, and if he dies I'll come to his house like a good kinsman and bring a calf from his calf."

Crooked Arm's relative, on learning of these terms, is said to have taken offence and told the messenger to tell Crooked Arm without any hints this time that he did not want any calf from his calf, and certainly not when he himself was dead; he wanted his own calf, while he was still alive, the calf which he had brought to the funeral as an offering as a good kinsman should. Since Crooked Arm still had not died it was time to return the calf to its proper owner. Moreover, he gave his word that in spite of the fact that while he was at Crooked Arm's house he had suffered the humiliation of being measured with a bit of string, he would nevertheless, if Crooked Arm really did die, bring the calf back again.

"This man will drive me to the grave with that calf of

his," is what Crooked Arm is supposed to have said on hearing these explanations. "Tell him," he added, "that he has not long to wait now, so it's not worth tormenting the wretched animal."

A few days after this conversation Crooked Arm transplanted from his allotment to his grave two young peach trees. Possibly he did this to revive the idea of his imminent doom. Yashka and I helped him. But apparently the two young peach trees were not enough for him. Some days later he went to the farm plantation at night, dug up a small tung tree and planted it between the two peach trees. Everyone soon got to know about this. The members of the farm chuckled among themselves and said that Crooked Arm wanted to poison the dead with the tung fruit. No one attached much importance to the transplanting because no one before or since had ever stolen a tung tree for the simple reason that no peasant farmer had any use for one, the fruit of the tung being deadly poisonous and consequently rather dangerous.

The former owner of the calf also fell silent. Either he became convinced that Crooked Arm was doomed after having planted a tung tree on his grave, or else, fearing the old man's tongue, which was no less venomous than the tung fruit, he had decided to leave him in peace.

Incidentally, legend has it that it was Crooked Arm's tongue in his young days that gave him his crooked arm. It happened in the following manner.

They say that after some feast or other, the local prince was sitting surrounded by numerous guests in his host's courtyard. The prince was eating peaches, which he peeled with a small penknife attached to a silver chain. This penknife on its silver chain, by the way, has nothing to do with the subsequent events, but all narrators of this tale have mentioned this penknife, never failing to add that it was attached to a silver chain. In retelling the incident once again I should have liked to avoid that penknife on its silver chain, but for some reason I feel that I must mention it, that it contains some element of truth without which something will be lost — though I don't know what.

Anyway, the prince was eating peaches and complacently recalling amorous joys. In the end, so they say, he surveyed the host's courtyard and remarked with a sigh, "If I were to assemble all the women I have had in my time, this yard wouldn't hold them."

But Crooked Arm, they say, even in those days, despite his youth, never allowed anyone to be complacent for long. He popped up from somewhere and said, "I wonder how many she-asses there would be braying in this yard?"

This somewhat elderly prince was a great connoisseur of feminine beauty, added to which, they say, he was modestly proud of his ability to strip a fruit of its skin without once breaking the ribbon of peel. This skill never deserted him, not even after a night's hard drinking. No matter how closely he was watched, or how hard people tried to distract him, he never made a slip. Sometimes they would try to catch him out with a fruit of extremely odd and ugly shape, but he would examine it from all angles, take out his little penknife on its silver chain and unerringly set it to work along the only correct path.

Having thus produced a spiral wreath of peel, he would usually hold it up before the assembled company. And if there was a pretty girl among them he would call her over and hang the ring of peel over her ear.

It seems to me that Crooked Arm must have been irritated by the prince's skill. I think he must have been observing him for a long time and was sure that sooner or later the ribbon of peel would break. He may actually have placed great hopes in one particular peach, but the prince had, as usual, dealt with it quite successfully and even started boasting about his women. You must agree there was enough to make Crooked Arm explode, particularly as a young man.

They say that after Crooked Arm's unexpected remark the prince turned purple and stared speechlessly at him with his eyes popping out, still holding in his right hand the peeled and oozing peach, and in his left, the penknife on its silver chain.

Everyone was struck dumb with horror, but the prince continued to stare unblinkingly at Crooked Arm while the hand that was holding the peach moved restlessly in the

air as though sensing how inappropriate it was to be holding a peach at that moment, not to mention the difficulty of drawing a pistol while holding a peach in one's
hand, particularly a peeled one. They say his hand even
lowered to the ground to get rid of the peach, but at the
last moment somehow could not bring itself to do such
a thing. After all, the peach had been skinned and a well
brought-up princely hand must have felt that a skinned
peach simply could not be placed on the ground. And
so it rose again, this hand, and for an agonising second
groped in the air for an invisible plate, feeling that there
must be someone who would think of providing a plate,
but everyone was paralysed with fear and no one had the
presence of mind to help the prince discard this, by now
indecently naked peach. And at this point, they say,
Crooked Arm himself came to the prince's aid.

"Pop it in your mouth!" he suggested.

The guests had no time to recover from this fresh
impertinence before they found themselves witnessing the
inexplicable self-abasement of the prince, who is said
to have begun in shameful haste to push the juicy,
dripping peach into his mouth, while continuing to stare
at Crooked Arm with hate-filled eyes. At last, having
somehow coped with the peach, he reached for his
pistol. Still gazing at Crooked Arm with those bulging,
hate-filled eyes, he fumbled speechlessly in the region of
his belt but, owing to his extreme agitation, or, as others
infer more correctly, because his hands were sticky with
peach juice, he just could not unbutton his holster.

Perhaps someone would yet have come to his senses,
perhaps someone might have managed to seize the
prince's arm or, at least, hustle Crooked Arm aside,
making it impossible to shoot and perhaps dangerous for
other people, but then, they say, Shchaaban's voice rang
out in the silence for the last time. I don't mean in the sense that after this his voice never rang out any more. Rather on the contrary, it became even louder and more
scornful. But in the sense that after this phrase he ceased
to be just Shchaaban and became Shchaaban Crooked
Arm.

"I bet he doesn't take so long over the other thing,"

he is said to have remarked, "judging by the way our Chegem she-asses..."

They say he did not finish his remark about the she-asses because the old prince, at last, coped with his holster — a shot rang out, the women shrieked and, when the smoke cleared, Crooked Arm was what fate had destined him to be, that is, crooked-armed. Afterwards, when he was asked why after the first insult he had gone on teasing the prince he would simply reply, "I just couldn't stop."

Later on, however, when the prince went off with the Mensheviks and Soviet power was finally and irrevocably established in our part of the country, Crooked Arm began to assert that he had had an old score to settle with the prince, perhaps even something to do with the days of partisan warfare, and that this exchange had been merely a pretext for, or consequence of, other more important things.

In short, despite the prince's bullet, Crooked Arm went on taking the rise out of anyone and everyone and his jokes seemed to lose none of their sting as the years went by.

When I was roaming round the village I would often see him on the tobacco or tea plantation or weeding the maize. If he was in a good mood he would simply play the fool and have everyone doubled up with laughter.

He had a knack of imitating the voices of people he knew and of animals as well; and he was particularly good at crowing like a cock.

Sometimes he would jab his hoe into the ground, straighten his back, look around and let out a mighty crow. The cocks in the neighbouring yards would answer almost at once. Everyone would burst out laughing, and while the nearest cock went on calling him he would resume his hoeing and mutter, "A fat lot you know, you fool."

Down our way, like everywhere else probably, people believe that the crowing of a cock has a special meaning, that it is almost an omen of the owner's fate. Crooked Arm was debunking these rural clairvoyants. In spite of his half-withered arm he certainly worked like the devil. Although, when sometimes there was a rumour that a new national loan was being floated, to which contributions

121

would be required, or when the remaining men in the village were being mobilised for tree-felling, he would slip his left arm into a clean red sling and go about like that for as long as he considered necessary. I don't think this red sling was much help to him; it certainly couldn't get him out of signing up for the loan. Nonetheless, it apparently provided him with some additional pretext for argument.

I believe he acquired this red sling to give his arm a soldierly, partisan appearance. Whenever he was summoned by the management board he would put his arm in its sling before leaving. Mounted on horseback with a black sheepskin cloak draped over his shoulders and his arm in a red sling, he certainly did have the rather dashing air of the partisan fighter.

All was well in the village, when suddenly it became known that the chairman of the village Soviet had received an anonymous letter against Crooked Arm. The letter declared that the planting of a tung tree on a grave was an insult to this new industrial crop, a hint that the plant was of no use to living collective farmers, and that its proper place was in the village cemetery.

The chairman of the village Soviet showed this letter to the chairman of the collective farm, who, they say, was properly scared by it, because someone might think that he had given Crooked Arm the idea of transplanting the tung tree to his own grave.

In those days I just couldn't understand why things had taken such a threatening turn — after all, everyone had known before the letter was sent that Crooked Arm had planted the tung tree on his grave. In those days I didn't realise that a letter was a document, and a document had to be presented on demand, had to be answered for.

To be sure, some people say that the chairman of the village Soviet need not have passed it on, but that he had a grudge against Crooked Arm, and that was why he showed it to the chairman of the farm.

In short, the letter was set in motion and one day a man arrived from the district centre to find out the truth of the matter. Crooked Arm tried to laugh it off, but, so they say, he had clearly lost his nerve because afterwards he had a shave, put his arm in the red sling and went about the village staring at it as if it was just about to blow up and the only thing he and everyone else around could do would be to dodge the splinters.

"Now you've done it," said Mustafa, an old horseman, the friend and eternal rival of Crooked Arm. "Now you'd better guzzle your tung apples and jump into your grave, otherwise they'll pack you off to Siberia."

"I'm not afraid of Siberia. I'm afraid you'll step into my grave while I'm away," Crooked Arm replied.

"In Siberia, they say, they ride on dogs," Mustafa suggested meanly. "You'd better take a bridle with you and try breaking in a dog for yourself."

The long-standing rivalry between Crooked Arm and Mustafa was over horses and horsemanship. They both had their feats and failures behind them. Crooked Arm had covered himself with undying glory by stealing a famous stallion at a certain race meeting in full view of thousands of spectators (personally, I doubt whether there were thousands). They say that Crooked Arm had been mounted on such a wretched, broken-winded nag and had looked so pathetic that when he asked the owner of the stallion permission to put his famous race-horse through its paces, the latter had granted the permission as a joke, because he was sure the stallion would throw Crooked Arm right away and thus add still further to its renown.

Crooked Arm, they say, slithered awkwardly off his doleful jade and, as he passed the reins to the owner of the stallion, said, "Let's count it that we've swopped."

"Done," the owner replied, taking the reins from him.

"Whatever you do, don't let this one throw you first time, or he'll trample you to death," Crooked Arm warned him, and went over to the stallion.

"I'll be careful," the owner is said to have replied and, as soon as Crooked Arm mounted the stallion, gave a sign to a lad standing in the background, and the lad gave the stallion a tremendous whack with his whip.

The stallion reared and galloped off towards the River Kodor, and Crooked Arm, they say, hung on at first like a drunken mullah on a galloping donkey.

Everyone was expecting him to fall off, but he went on and on and the owner's jaw began to drop as Crooked Arm reached the end of the field and, instead of following the bend of the race-course, went careering on towards the river. For another few minutes they hesitated, thinking the horse had taken the bit between its teeth and he could not make it turn, but then they realised that this was a robbery of quite unprecedented daring. Fifteen minutes later a dozen horsemen were galloping in pursuit, but it was too late.

Crooked Arm had leapt headlong down the cliff to the river and by the time his pursuers reached the edge he was climbing out on the far bank; for an instant, the stallion's wet crupper gleamed in the alders at the water's edge. The bullets flew wide and no one dared take a flying leap down the cliff. Since then the spot has been known as Crooked Arm Cliff. Crooked Arm himself never told this story in my presence, but he allowed others to tell it, listening with pleasure and making a few corrections. He would always wink at Mustafa if he was present, and Mustafa would pretend not to be listening, until in the end he could not refrain from trying to belittle or ridicule the exploit.

Mustafa would say that a man with one arm shot through was disabled anyway, so he had not risked all that much for the sake of his exploit. And if he had jumped down the cliff he had done it, first, because he was scared and, secondly, because there was nothing else he could do, since he would have been shot dead in any case if he had been caught by his pursuers.

In short, there was a deep and long-standing rivalry between them. In their young days they used to thresh it out at the races; now, in old age, though they still kept horses, they solved their disputes theoretically, in the course of which they would become involved in a jungle of ominous-sounding riddles.

"If a man shoots at you from over there and you, say, are riding down that path, where would you turn your horse at the sound of the shot — and, mind you, there's not a single tree around?"

"Suppose you're galloping down a hill with someone

124

chasing you. Ahead on the right there's some scrub, and on the left there's a ravine. Where do you turn your horse then?"

Such were the disputes these two men would hold as they trudged home with hoes or axes on their shoulders, after a long day's work.

These disputes had been going on for many years, although it was a long time since anyone had done any shooting round our way, and certainly not at these old men, for people had learned how to avenge an insult by safer methods. And to one of these methods, namely, the anonymous letter, it is now time for us to return.

The representative from the district centre tried to make the old man say what his real purpose had been in moving the tung tree, and, above all, to reveal who had instigated him to do so. Crooked Arm replied that no one had instigated him, that he himself had suddenly wanted to have a tung tree growing at his head when he lay dead and buried, because he had long since taken a fancy to this plant that till recently had been quite unknown in our district. The man from the centre did not believe him.

Then Crooked Arm confessed he had been relying on the poisonous properties not only of the fruit but of the roots of the tree; he had been hoping that its roots would kill all the grave worms and he would lie in peace and cleanliness, because he had had enough trouble from the fleas in this world.

But at this point, they say, the man from the centre asked what he meant by fleas. Crooked Arm replied that by fleas he means dog's fleas, which should not be confused with poultry lice, which did not worry him in the least, any more than buffalo ticks did. But if there was one thing that he couldn't stand it was the horse flies, and if he did throw a couple of handfuls of superphosphate under a horse's tail during the heat of the day, it was no great loss to the collective farm and the horse had a rest from the flies. The man from the centre realised that he couldn't draw blood there either, so he went back to the subject of the tung.

In short, no matter what excuses Crooked Arm produced, things began to look black for him. The next day he was not even summoned before the comrade from the district centre. Ready for anything, he sat in the yard of the management office in the shade of a mulberry tree and, keeping his arm in the red sling all the time, smoked and waited for his fate to be decided. Then it was, they say, that Mustafa turned up and walked straight into the management office, where the chairman of the collective farm, the chairman of the village Soviet and the man from the district centre were conferring together. As he walked past Crooked Arm, he looked at him and said, "I've thought of something. If it doesn't help, you'd better lie down quietly in your grave, just as you are, with your sling on, and I'll shake some tung fruit down on you."

Crooked Arm made no reply to these words. He merely glanced sadly at his arm as much as to say that he was ready to put up with any amount of suffering but why should his arm, which had already suffered enough from the Menshevik's bullet, suffer again?

Mustafa had a great reputation with the local authorities for being the shrewdest man on the farm. His house was the biggest and finest in the village, so if any top people came to visit us they were promptly dispatched to Mustafa's hospitable house.

What Mustafa had thought of was splendidly simple. The man from the centre was an Abkhazian, and if a man is an Abkhazian, even if he has come from Ethiopia, he is bound to have relatives in Abkhazia.

That night, apparently, Mustafa had secretly assembled all the old men of the village at his house, dined them and wined them, and with their help thoroughly investigated the family origins of the comrade from the district centre. Careful and all-round analysis had shown quite clearly that the comrade from the district centre was through his great aunt, once a town girl and now living in the village of Merkheul, related by blood to my Uncle Meksut. Mustafa was quite satisfied with the results of this analysis.

With this trump card in his pocket he marched past Crooked Arm into the management office. They say that when Mustafa informed the comrade from the district cen-

126

tre of this fact, the latter turned pale and began to deny his being related to the great aunt from Merkheul village and particularly to Uncle Meksut. But the trap had worked. Mustafa merely laughed at his denials and said, "If he's not a relative of yours, why are you so pale?"

He said no more and left the office.

"What shall I do?" Crooked Arm asked when he saw Mustafa.

"Wait till evening," Mustafa replied.

"Make up your mind soon," Crooked Arm said, "or my arm will wither away altogether in this sling."

"Till evening," Mustafa repeated, and walked off.

The fact of the matter was that in denying his relationship with Uncle Meksut the comrade from the district centre had mortally insulted my uncle. But Uncle Meksut kept his temper. Without saying a word to anyone he merely saddled his horse and rode away to the village of Merkheul.

By evening he returned on his sweating mount, reined up at the management office, and handed the bridle to Old Crooked Arm, who was still waiting there in suspense. The chairman was standing on the veranda, smoking and surveying Crooked Arm and the surrounding scenery.

"Come in," the chairman said at the sight of Uncle Meksut.

"Just a minute," Uncle Meksut replied and, before mounting the steps, ripped the red sling off the old man's arm and tucked it without a word into his pocket.

They say the old man just stood there with his arm suspended in midair, as though unable to comprehend this symbolic gesture.

Uncle Meksut placed in front of the comrade from the district centre the yellowed, crumbling birth certificate of his great aunt of Merkheul, issued by the notary public's office of the Sukhumi *uyezd* in the days before the revolution. At the sight of this birth certificate the comrade from the district centre, they say, again turned pale, but could no longer offer any denials.

"Or shall I bring you your great aunt here over my saddle bow?" Uncle Meksut asked him.

"You needn't do that," the comrade from the district

centre answered very quietly.

"Will you take your brief-case with you or put it in the safe?" Uncle Meksut asked.

"I'll take it with me," the comrade replied.

"Come along then," Uncle Meksut said and they left the office.

That evening there was a party at Uncle Meksut's house and the whole case was considered. The next morning after a long discussion in Uncle Meksut's house a statement was drawn up in Russian-Caucasian officialese and dictated to me personally.

"At last this parasite has come in useful," Crooked Arm said, when I moved the inkstand towards me and sat poised to take the dictation.

The leaders of the collective farm discussed the statement with the comrade from the district centre. Crooked Arm listened attentively and asked for every phrase to be translated into the Abkhazian language. Moreover, he made several amendments to the wording which, as I realise now, were designed to enhance his social and practical merits.

The passage dealing with his crooked arm gave rise to particularly furious disputes. Crooked Arm demanded that it should be stated that he had suffered from the bullet of a Menshevik hireling in view of the fact that the prince who had wounded him had afterwards gone off with the Mensheviks. The comrade from the district centre clutched his temples and begged them to stick to the facts because he also had to answer to his superiors, even though he did respect his relatives. In the end they arrived at a version that satisfied everyone.

The statement took so long to draft that while I was writing it down in my wavering hand I actually learned it off by heart. Its authors asked me to read it out loud, which I did with great feeling. After this it was given to the secretary of the village Soviet to be copied. This is what it said:

"The old man Shchaaban Larba, otherwise known as Crooked Arm, a nickname he acquired some time before the revolution together with a prince's bullet, which later turned out to be a Menshevik bullet, has ever since the organisation of the collective farm worked actively on the farm in spite of the handicap of his partly withered arm (left).

"The old man Shchaaban Larba, otherwise known as Crooked Arm, has a son who at the present time is fighting at the front in the Patriotic War and has won government decorations (field post-office number indicated in brackets).

"The old man Shchaaban Larba, otherwise known as Crooked Arm, despite his advanced age, is in these difficult times working without respite in the collectivised fields, giving his above-mentioned arm no rest. Every year he does the equivalent of not less than four hundred work-day units.

"The collective farm management together with the chairman of the village Soviet affirms that, being a pre-revolutionary and uneducated old man, he transplanted the said tung tree to the site of his fictitious grave by mistake, for which he will be fined in accordance with collective farm regulations. The management of the collective farm affirms that the transplantation of tung trees from collective farm plantations to the communal cemetery and particularly to home allotments has never been practised on a mass scale and is in the nature of an individual lapse of consciousness.

"The collective farm management affirms that old man Shchaaban Larba, otherwise known as Crooked Arm, has never poured scorn on collective farm affairs but in accordance with his gay and peppery character (Abkhazian pepper) has poured scorn on certain individuals, which include quite a few parasites of the collective farm fields, who are heroes in quotation marks and advanced workers, without quotation marks, on their own home allotments. But we have been eradicating such heroes and advanced workers and shall continue to do so in accordance with the collective farm regulations up to and including expulsion from the collective farm and confiscation of home allotments.

"The old man Shchaaban Larba, thanks to his inborn folk talent, mimicks the local cocks, in the course of which he exposes the most harmful Moslem customs of olden

129

times and also entertains the collective farmers without interrupting work in the fields."

The statement was signed and sealed by the chairman of the collective farm and the chairman of the village Soviet.

When the work was done, the guests went out on to the veranda, where farewell glasses of *Isabella* were drunk and the comrade from the district centre passed a hint through one of the members of the management board that he would not be averse to listening to Crooked Arm mimicking the cocks. Crooked Arm did not have to be asked twice. He raised his immortal hand to his mouth and gave such a cock-a-doodle-doo that all the cocks in the vicinity broke loose like dogs from the chain. Only the host's cock, before whose very eyes the whole deception took place, was at first struck dumb with indignation, and then burst into such a fit of crowing that it had to be chased out of the yard on to the vegetable patch because it offended the ear of the comrade from the district centre and prevented him from making himself heard.

"Does it work on all cocks or only on the local ones?" the comrade from the district centre asked, having waited for the cock to be chased out of hearing.

"On all of them," Crooked Arm replied readily. "Try it out anywhere you like."

"A real folk artist," said the comrade from the district centre, and everyone started saying goodbye to Uncle Meksut, who accompanied them to the gate and a little further.

The chairman of the collective farm carried out to the letter what had been promised in the statement. He fined Crooked Arm twenty work-day units. In addition, he ordered him to move the tung tree back to the plantation and to fill in the grave forever as a precaution against accidents to cattle. Crooked Arm dug up the tree and moved it to the plantation, but its sufferings had been too great and it declined into a half-withered state.

"Like my arm," said Crooked Arm. But he managed to defend his grave by surrounding it with a rather handsome stake fence with a gate and a latch.

After the business of the anonymous letter had died down Crooked Arm's relative once again, through an intermediary, cautiously reminded him about the calf.

Crooked Arm replied that he couldn't be bothered with the calf just now because he had been disgraced and slandered, and was busy day and night looking for the slanderer and even took his gun with him to work. He would know no peace until he had driven the slanderer into his grave and would not even grudge him his own grave if he was not too big for it. Finally, he wanted his relative to keep his ear to the ground and his eyes peeled so that at the slightest suspicion he could give Crooked Arm the signal and Crooked Arm would know what to do. Only when he had fulfilled his Manly Duty would he be able to settle the business of the calf and other minor misunderstandings that were quite natural between relatives.

After that, they say, the relative fell silent altogether and never mentioned the calf again and tried to keep out of Crooked Arm's way. None the less they did run into one another at a celebration of some kind. It was late at night and Crooked Arm had plenty of drink inside him, and during the performance of a drinking song that allowed of some improvisation, he started repeating the same couplet over and over again:

> O, raida, siua raida, ei,
> Who sold his kinsman for a calf...

He went on singing without looking in the direction of his relative, with the result that the latter gradually became sober and in the end, unable to bear it any longer, asked Crooked Arm across the table:

"What are you trying to say?"

"Nothing," Crooked Arm replied, and looked at him as though taking his measurements, "just singing."

"Yes, but it's a funny kind of song," said the relative. "In our village everyone sings it except one man."

"What man?" the relative asked.

"Guess," Crooked Arm suggested.

"I wouldn't even try," the relative said hastily.

"Then I'll tell you," Crooked Arm threatened.

"Go on, then!" the relative challenged recklessly.

"The chairman of the village Soviet," declared Crooked Arm.

"Why doesn't he sing it?" the relative asked pointblank.

"He's not allowed to drop hints," Crooked Arm explained.

"Can you prove anything?" the relative asked.

"No, I can't, so for the time being I'm just singing," said Crooked Arm and once again surveyed the relative, as though taking his measurements.

By this time they had attracted the anxious attention of their host, who did not want them to spoil the feast he was giving to celebrate the decoration of his son with the Order of the Red Banner.

Again someone struck up the song and everyone sang, and Crooked Arm sang with the others without any particular variations because he felt the host's eye upon him. But when the host relaxed, Crooked Arm seized his chance, and invented another line:

O, raida, siua raida, ei,
With a fence the dear one is protected...

But the host did hear him nevertheless and came over to the two men with a horn full of wine.

"Crooked Arm!" he cried. "Swear by our sons who are shedding their blood in the country's defence that you will be forever reconciled at this table."

"I've forgotten about the calf," the relative said.

"And high time you did," Crooked Arm corrected him, then turned to the host: "For the sake of our children I'd eat dirt — be it as you wish. Amen!"

And he threw back his head and drank a litre horn of wine in a single draught, leaning further and further back to the accompaniment of a general chorus helping him to drink: "Uro, uro, uro, u-r-o-o..."

Then the whole table again burst into song and the relative, so they say, waited anxiously to see how he would sing the passage that could be improvised. And when Crooked Arm sang:

> *O, raida, siua raida, ei,*
> *O heroes, advancing under fire...*

the relative listened intently for a few seconds, considering the words from all points of view, and finally, having decided that he bore no resemblance whatever to a hero advancing under fire, felt entirely relieved and joined in the singing.

In the autumn we gathered a rich harvest from our allotment and returned to town with maize, pumpkins, nuts and an enormous quantity of dried fruit. In addition, we had laid in a store of about twenty bottles of *bekmez*, fruit honey; in this case, made of apples.

We had struck a bargain with one of the workteam leaders on the farm that we would pick the apples in an old orchard, giving half the harvest to the farm and keeping the other half for ourselves.

Because of the shortage of labour at the farm there was simply no one to pick the apples; everyone was busy with the main crops — tea, tobacco and tung.

Having obtained permission to pick the apples, mother in her turn struck a bargain with three soldiers in a battalion stationed close by that they would help us to pick, crush and boil the *bekmez* out of the apples and in exchange receive half of our half of the harvest.

In a week the operation was brilliantly completed. We acquired twenty bottles of thick golden *bekmez* (clear profit), which provided us with a substitute for sugar for the whole of the next winter.

Thus, having given everyone a splendid lesson in commercial enterprise, we left the collective farm and Crooked Arm's voice faded away into the distance.

* * *

Many years later, during a hunting trip I again found myself in that village.

While waiting for a passing lorry to give me a lift, I stood outside the management office in the shade of the same old mulberry tree. It was a hot August day. I looked at the deserted school building, at the school yard covered with succulent grass, grass of oblivion for me, at the eucalyptus trees that we had once planted, at the old gymnastics bar which we used to make a dash for every break between lessons, and with a traditional sense of sorrow I breathed the fragrance of years gone by.

Occasional passers-by greeted me as everyone does in the country, but none of them recognised me, nor I them. A girl came out of the office carrying two water bottles, lazily let the bucket down the well and filled it. Slowly she wound the bucket up again and started filling both bottles at once, splashing water over them as though taking a delight in the sudden abundance of cool. Then she tipped out the rest of the water on the grass and walked lazily back to the office, carrying the wet bottles.

When she mounted the steps and went in through the door I heard the wave of voices rise to meet her, and suddenly subside as the door closed. A feeling came over me that this had all happened before.

A lad wearing a jacket and with one leg of his trousers rolled up, rode past me on a rustily squeaking bicycle, then turned round, his thoughts still riveted on something else, and rode up to me to ask for a light.

He had two large loaves of bread tied to his carrier. I gave him a light and asked him if he knew Yashka, the grandson of Crooked Arm.

"Of course, I do," he replied. "Yashka the postman. Just wait here. He'll soon be coming along on his motor-bike."

I started watching the road and quite soon I did hear the chugging of a motor-cycle. I recognised Yashka only because I was expecting him. On his lightweight mount he looked like Gulliver on a children's bicycle.

"Yashka!" I shouted. He looked in my direction and the motor-cycle came to a startled halt, then he seemed to press it down into the earth and the engine gave up altogether.

Yashka wheeled the bike out from under him. We walked away from the road and in about fifteen minutes were lying in dense fern thickets.

A big, burly fellow, with a lazy smile on his face, he lay beside me, still very much like the Yashka who used to sit behind his grandfather on horseback and gaze absent-mindedly around him. Until a short while ago, apparently, he had been one of the farm's team-leaders but he had slipped up somewhere and had now been given the job of postman. He told me this with the same lazy smile. Even at school it had been obvious that ambition was not one of his weaknesses.

His grandfather, it seems, had expended the whole supply of family frenzy himself, so that there just was nothing left for Yashka to work himself into a frenzy with. What difference did it make whether he was a team-leader or a postman, a postman or a team-leader? His voice, however, seemed as deep and powerful as his grandfather's, but without those choking high notes. I asked him, of course, about his grandfather.

"You mean to say you never heard?" Yashka asked in surprise, and stared at me with his big round eyes.

"Heard what?" I asked.

"But everyone knows about that affair. Where have you been?"

"In Moscow," I said.

"Ah, so it hasn't got to Moscow," Yashka drawled, expressing his respect for the distance between Abkhazia and Moscow; if a story like that had not reached Moscow yet, it really must be a very long way.

Yashka raked in some more fern and packed it under him, settled his head more comfortably on his postman's bag and told me about his indefatigable grandfather's last adventure. I heard the story later from several other people, but the first person to tell me was Yashka.

I was still marvelling at this, the final mighty splash of Old Crooked Arm's imagination, when all of a sudden...

"Zhuzhuna! Zhuzhuna!" Yashka called out without so much as a pause after his story, and not even raising his head from the ground.

"What's the matter?" a girl's voice responded from somewhere. I raised myself on my elbow and looked round. Beyond the fern thickets there was a small beech grove. Through the trees I made out a fence and, beyond that, a field of maize. The voice had come from there.

"There's a letter for you, Zhuzhuna! A letter!" Yashka called again, and winked at me.

"Are you making it up?" I whispered.

Yashka nodded joyfully and listened. The hushed grasshoppers cautiously began buzzing to each other again.

"Humbug!" the girl's voice rang out at last, and I sensed that the postman's ruse had flushed the hind.

"Hurry up, Zhuzhuna, hurry, or I'll be gone!" Yashka called delightedly, intoxicated either with the sound of his own voice or by the sound of the girl's name.

I realised it was time for me to go and began to say goodbye. Still listening for reply, Yashka urged me to stay the night but I refused; both because I was in a hurry and because, if I did so, I would offend my own folk, whom I had not been to see. I knew that if I stayed the night there would be no hunting trip for me, because it would take me another two days to recover.

As I made my way up the path to the road I again heard the girl's voice; now it sounded more distinct.

"Tell me who it's from — then I'll come!" she was calling invitingly.

"Come, and then I'll tell you, Zhuzhuna, Zhuzhuna!" floated back on the hot August air for the last time, and with a vague sense of melancholy or, to put it more plainly, envy, I stepped out into the deserted village street.

Well, anyway, I thought, Old Crooked Arm's traditions are not dying out. Half an hour later I left the village and have not been there since; but I still hope to go and pay our folk a visit, if only to find out where Yashka's shouts got him with his Zhuzhuna.

* * *

I will tell Crooked Arm's last adventure as I now have it in my head.

Crooked Arm had lived to see the end of the war and the return of his son and had gone on living splendidly until quite recently. But a year or so ago, the time had come for him to die, and this time it was the real thing.

That day he was, as usual, lying on the veranda of his house and watching his horse grazing in the yard when Mustafa rode up. Mustafa dismounted and walked up the steps on to the veranda. A chair was brought out for him and he sat down beside Crooked Arm. As usual, they recalled times gone by. Crooked Arm would lapse for an instant into forgetfulness or doze, but as soon as he awoke he would always resume from exactly where he had left off.

"So you're really leaving us?" Mustafa asked, with a sharp glance at his friend and rival.

"Yes, I am," Crooked Arm replied. "I'll soon be bathing the other world's horses in the other world's rivers."

"We'll all be there one day," Mustafa sighed politely. "But I didn't think you'd be the first."

"There were other times when you didn't think I'd be first, at the races," Crooked Arm said so clearly that the relatives waiting at his bedside all heard him and even had a little laugh, although they concealed it with their hands, because it was not quite appropriate to laugh in the presence of a dying man, even if that man happened to be Crooked Arm.

Mustafa felt slighted, but it would have been impolite to argue, because the man was dying. And yet, it was somehow particularly humiliating for a man who was alive and well to be laughed at by a dying man, because if a dying man laughed at you, it meant you must be in an even more disastrous or pitiful state than he — and how much worse could that be!

It would, of course, have been impolite to argue, but at least one could tell a story. So he told one.

"As you're going away on this journey, I had better tell you something," Mustafa said, bending over Crooked Arm.

"Tell me then, if you must," Crooked Arm replied, not looking round because he was watching the yard, where his horse was grazing. In the time left to him his greatest interest was in watching his horse.

"Don't be angry, Crooked Arm, but it was I who rang up the farm and told them you had died," Mustafa said, as though sorrowing that circumstances did not permit him now, as then, to launch that false rumour again, and wishing it to be understood that he regretted this as a true friend should.

"How could you, when they spoke Russian?" Crooked Arm asked in surprise and looked at him.

Mustafa knew no Russian and, in spite of his great managerial talents, was so illiterate that he had been obliged to invent his own alphabet or, at least, introduce for his own use certain quaint hieroglyphs with the help of which he kept a note of all the people who were in debt to him, and also a set of accounts based on complex, multi-stage barter operations. So, naturally, Crooked Arm was surprised to hear of his speaking on the telephone, particularly in Russian.

"Through my nephew in town. I was standing beside him," Mustafa explained. "As they had cured you I decided to have a joke, and besides who would have sent a lorry for you but for that," he added, recalling the difficulties of those far-off days.

They say Crooked Arm closed his eyes and for a long time was silent. Then he slowly opened them again and said without looking at Mustafa:

"Now I see you are a better horseman than I am."

"It looks like it," Mustafa admitted modestly and glanced round at those who were attending the dying man.

But at this point the close relatives gave way to tears because it was the first time in his life that Crooked Arm had ever acknowledged himself beaten, and this was more like death than death itself that was so near.

Crooked Arm silenced them and nodded in the direction of the horses.

"Give them some water. They're thirsty."

One of the girls took two pails and went for water. She came back with the pails full of clear spring water and placed them in the middle of the yard. Crooked Arm's horse went up to one of the pails and began to drink, and Mustafa's horse turned its head and pulled at the halter. The girl untethered the horse and, holding the bridle, stood by while it drank. The horses reached down with their long necks, drinking quietly, and Crooked Arm watched them with pleasure, and his Adam's apple, they say, moved up and down as though he himself were drinking.

"Mustafa," he said at length, turning to his friend, "now I admit that you knew more about horses than I did, but you know that I loved horses and had some understanding of them."

"But, of course! Who doesn't know that!" Mustafa exclaimed generously, and again turned round to look at everyone who was on the veranda.

"In a few days I shall die," Crooked Arm continued. "My coffin will stand where those empty pails are standing now. When the weeping is over, I want you to do something for me."

"What is it?" Mustafa asked, and with a hiss at the members of the family, because they had again tried to sob, bent over his friend. It looked as if Crooked Arm was expressing his last will.

"I want you to take your horse and jump three times over my coffin. Before they put the lid down I want to feel the smell of a horse over me. Will you do that?"

"I will, if our customs see in this no sin," Mustafa promised.

"I don't think they do," Crooked Arm said a little more slowly and closed his eyes — either he had fallen asleep or was just musing. Mustafa rose and walked quietly down from the veranda. He rode away, considering the last will of the dying man.

That evening Mustafa gathered the elders of the village, gave them all plenty to eat and drink and told them of Crooked Arm's request. The elders discussed the matter and reached a decision.

"You'd better jump, if that's his dying wish, because you're the best horseman now."

"He admitted that himself," Mustafa interpolated.

"There's no sin in it because a horse doesn't eat meat and its breath is clean," they concluded.

Crooked Arm heard of the elders' decision the same night and, so they say, was well pleased. Two days later he died.

Once again, as during the war, the messengers of woe were sent out to the neighbouring villages. Some received the news of his death with suspicion, and the relative who had brought the calf in those days said that it would do no harm to jab him with the sharp end of a crook to make sure he really was dead and not just shamming.

"There's no need to jab him," the messenger of woe replied patiently, "because horseman Mustafa is going to jump over him. That was his dying wish."

"Then I'll go," the relative said with relief. "Crooked Arm wouldn't let anyone jump over him while he was still alive."

They say there were even more people at the funeral this time than before, when no one had any doubt that Crooked Arm was dead. Many of them, of course, were attracted by the promised spectacle of a funeral steeple-chase. They all knew of the great rivalry between the two friends, and it was said that even though Crooked Arm was dead he wouldn't let the matter rest there.

Afterwards some people claimed to have seen Mustafa practising in his yard with a trough propped on chairs. But Mustafa denied with a frenzy worthy of Crooked Arm himself that he had been jumping over any such trough. He said his horse could easily leap a gate if necessary and Crooked Arm wouldn't be able to reach him even if he tried to do so with his famous arm.

And so, on the fourth day after the old man's death, when everyone had finished taking final leave of their relative and fellow villager, Mustafa stationed himself by the coffin, awaiting his finest hour, sorrowful and at the same time impatient.

When the time came he delivered a short speech, full of a solemn dignity. He recounted the heroic life of Shchaaban Larba, otherwise known as Crooked Arm, from one horse to the next, right up to his dying wish. As a brief reminder to the young, Mustafa mentioned the feat of the stolen stallion and how Crooked Arm had not been afraid to leap down the cliff, giving it to be understood in passing that if he had yielded to fear it would have been a great deal worse for him. He said that he recalled the incident not in order to detract from Crooked Arm's exploit but to offer the young folk yet another proof of the advantage of bold decisions.

And then, in accordance with the dead man's wish, and his own wish, he addressed the assembled elders in a thunderous voice and again asked them if it were not wicked to jump over a coffin.

"There is no sin in that," the elders replied. "A horse eats no meat, so its breath is clean."

After that Mustafa walked to the tethering post, untied his horse, leapt into the saddle, flourished his whip and charged along the corridor formed by the crowd towards the coffin.

While he had been walking to the tethering post the space beyond the coffin had been cleared and the people moved back so that the horse should not ride anyone down. Someone had suggested covering the dead man with the tent cape to protect him from any earth that might be scattered from the horse's hooves. But one of the elders had said there would be no sin in that either because he was going to lie in the earth anyway.

Well, Mustafa's horse charged up to the coffin and suddenly stopped dead. Mustafa shouted and lashed it on both flanks with his whip. The horse twisted its head round and bared its teeth, but stubbornly refused to jump.

Mustafa swung it round, galloped back, dismounted, for some reason tested the saddle girths, and once again swooped on the coffin like a hawk. But again the horse balked and, no matter how Mustafa whipped it, refused to jump, although it did rear.

There was about a minute of tense silence in which only the crack of the whip and Mustafa's laboured breathing could be heard.

And then one of the elders said:

"It strikes me the horse won't jump over a dead man."

"That's right," recalled one of the others. "A good dog won't bite his master's hand and a good horse won't jump over a dead man."

"Down you get, Mustafa," somebody shouted. "Crooked Arm has proved to you that he knew more about horses than you."

Mustafa turned his horse and, parting the crowd as he went, rode out of the yard. And then a tremendous burst of laughter went up among the mourners, such as one would be unlikely to hear even at a wedding, let alone a funeral.

The laughter was so loud and long that when the chairman of the village Soviet heard it in his office he dropped his rubber stamp and exclaimed:

"Upon my word, I believe Crooked Arm has jumped out of his grave at the last moment!"

It was a merry funeral. The next day Crooked Arm's posthumous joke was being told and retold in nearly every corner of Abkhazia. In the evening Mustafa was somehow persuaded to attend the funeral supper, for though it was no sin to jump over a dead man it was considered a sin to bear a grudge against the dead.

When an old man dies in our country the funeral feast is a lively affair. Men drink wine and tell each other funny stories. Custom forbids only drinking to excess and the singing of songs. Someone may inadvertently strike up a drinking song, but he is soon stopped and falls into an embarrassed silence.

It seems to me that when an old man dies there is place for merry-making and ritual splendour at his funeral feast. A man has completed life's journey and, if he dies in old age, having lived his span, it means there is cause for the living to celebrate his victory over fate.

And ritual splendour, if it is not taken to the absurd, did not spring from nowhere. It says to us: something tremendous has happened — a man has died. And if he was a good man, there will be many who wish to mark and remember the event. And who deserves to be remembered of men, if not Crooked Arm, who all his life enriched the earth with labour and merriment, and in his last ten years, it might be said, actually tended his own grave and made it bear fruit and gathered from it quite a good crop of peaches. You must agree that not everyone manages to pick a crop of peaches from his own grave; many may try but they lack the imagination and daring that Old Crooked Arm possessed.

And may the earth be soft as swan's down for him, as indeed it should be, considering that it was a good dry spot they chose for him, a fact he was very fond of mentioning while he lived.

BORROWERS

The man who wants to touch you for a loan sends no telegram in advance. Everything happens suddenly.

He begins by discussing certain cultural matters of wide general interest, possibly even outer space, listens to all you have to say on the subject with the greatest attention and, when a warm human relationship has developed between you in this abstract sphere, he takes advantage of the first pause in the conversation to splash down gently from the cosmic heights, and say:

"Incidentally, you couldn't lend me a tenner for a fortnight, could you?"

Such a swift change of subject cripples the imagination and always leaves me at a loss. What I really cannot understand is why this should be incidental. But that is the way of borrowers. They can turn any incident to their advantage.

For the first few precious seconds I am confused. And confusion spells disaster. The mere fact of not answering promptly indicates that I have money, and once that is established, it is the hardest thing in the world to prove that you need that money yourself. The only thing to do is to fork out.

Of course, there are some odd characters who pay back what they borrow. Actually they do a lot of harm. If they didn't exist, the whole tribe of chronic defaulters would have died out long ago. But, as things are, it continues to prosper, profiting by the moral credit of these eccentrics.

I did once refuse an obvious cadger. But I soon repented.

We met in a café. I might never have noticed him but for a revolting male habit I have of observing other people's tables. Our eyes happened to meet and I had to say hullo. It had seemed to me that he was firmly enough established at his own table. But he relinquished it with unexpected ease and, smiling joyfully, headed in my direction.

"Hullo, chum! How's the old country?" he bellowed from a distance.

I put on a stern expression but it was too late. There are some people you need only ask for a light and they'll be addressing you as "chum" and talking about "the old country" for the rest of your life.

I decided to allow no familiarity whatever and certainly none of his hail-fellow-well-met stuff. He fairly soon exhausted his wretched assortment of softening-up devices and in an offhand manner popped the fateful question.

"I'm out of cash," I said with a sigh, and made a rather feeble pretence of slapping my pockets, actually tapping my purse in doing so. The would-be borrower looked depressed. I rejoiced at having shown firmness and, in a sudden desire to palliate my refusal, found myself saying, "Of course, if you are very badly in need, I could borrow some from a friend."

"That's fine," he perked up immediately. "Why don't you give him a ring? I don't mind waiting."

He sat down at my table. Events were moving in a direction I had not foreseen.

"He lives a long way from here," I said, trying to damp his unexpected enthusiasm and restore the original state of depression.

"That's all right," he replied airily, refusing to have his enthusiasm damped or to succumb to his former dispiritedness. "I'll have a cup of coffee while I'm waiting." And he took a cigarette from the packet I had left lying on the table, as though surrendering himself entirely to my care.

"But I've just ordered a meal," I said, unconsciously switching to defence.

"You'll be there and back before they serve you. And if the worst comes to the worst, I can eat it and you'll order another one."

In short, the battle was lost. It's no use trying to fight

144

nature. If you haven't the gift for impromptu lying, it's better not to try.

I had to leave that warm café and go out into the slushy street. There wasn't really anyone to ring up but I went round the corner and slipped into a telephone booth.

I spent about fifteen minutes in that booth. First I took the required sum of money out of my purse and put it in one pocket, then I took out the cost of the meal and put that in another pocket. When I restored the purse to its usual place, it was nearly empty.

After this I returned slowly to the café, trying to read some newspapers that were on display in the street. But nothing I read made any sense because I was afraid of mixing up my pockets and bringing down on my own head this whole edifice of lies, whose stability always proves to be an illusion in the long run.

By the time I got back to the café he had finished off my dinner and was about to start on my coffee. I gave him the money and he put it in his pocket without counting it. I realised at once that its return journey to my pocket would be hard and long. It was.

"I've ordered you some coffee," he said considerately. "They're bringing it now."

There was nothing for me to do but drink the coffee because my appetite had quite disappeared. The waitress brought the coffee and the bill with it. When I had paid for my dinner, which he had eaten, he gave her a generous tip, as if to make up for my churlishness while he himself presented an image of bored but noble opulence.

Yes, all borrowers are like that. They usher you into a taxi, allowing you to enter first and exit last, so as not to get in your way while you are paying.

Shakespeare said that loan oft loses both itself and friend. My experience was the opposite, or rather, I certainly lost my money but I gained a dubious kind of friend.

One day I told him that everyone is in Great Debt to society. He agreed with me. Then I added cautiously that the concept of Great Debt is in fact made up of a multitude of small debts, which we are obliged to honour, even if at times they may appear onerous. But with this he would

145

not agree. He observed that the concept of Great Debt is not a multitude of small debts but, on the contrary, a Great Debt with capital letters, which one cannot fritter away without running the risk of becoming a vulgariser. What was more, he detected in my understanding of Great Debt certain traces of the theory of small deeds, which had long since been condemned by progressive Russian critics. I decided that the cost of reducing this fortress would exceed any tribute I might exact when it was conquered, and left him in peace.

But now here is a remarkable fact. It is easier to refuse a loan to the scrupulously honest than to people with what I would call a mini-conscience. When we refuse the former we comfort ourselves with the thought that our refusal is not motivated by the fear of losing money.

Life is much more difficult with habitual spongers. When we lend to them we know that we risk losing our money, and they know that we know the risk we are taking. This gives rise to a delicate situation. Our refusal appears to undermine the man's reputation. We insult him by treating him as a potential extortioner.

About one man who borrowed off me I have a longer tale to tell. I will not conceal the fact that besides the purely abstract aim of research I want to use this story to make good some of my philanthropic losses and also to scare some other borrowers with the possibility of exposure in print. There are not really so many of them. Out of a population of over two hundred million, only about seven or eight altogether. Only a tiny percentage, in fact. And yet how pleasant to know that you have awakened someone's conscience while at the same time recovering your long-lost money. If you ask me, there's nothing more timely than an unexpectedly repaid debt, and nothing more unexpected than a debt repaid on time. That's not such a bad phrase, is it? On the whole, I find that when we start talking about our losses, our voices acquire a note of genuine inspiration.

It all began when I received at a certain place quite a large sum of money. I won't say what place it was because you wouldn't be able to get anything there in any case.

Succumbing to the general craze, I decided to acquire

my own means of transport. I rejected the idea of a car at once. For one thing, you have to have a licence. Well, of course, some people buy licences. But that, I think, is just silly. First you buy a car, then a licence, and one day you have an accident and lose both the car and the licence, if you have the luck to get off so lightly. Besides, I had only about a fifth of the money needed to buy a car.

For all of these reasons I gave up the idea of owning a car. From the four-wheeled vehicle of my imagination I removed one wheel and the result was a comfortable three-wheeled motor-cycle and sidecar.

After mature reflection, however, I decided that a motor-cycle and sidecar would not suit me either, because of its incurable lack of symmetry. I knew that this lopsidedness would irritate me, and that in the end I should have to dispose of the sidecar with the aid of a roadside post.

Eventually I plumped for a bicycle and bought one. I found it had all kinds of advantages. A bicycle is the lightest, the quietest and the most reliable means of transport. What was more, I would be saving on petrol because its motive power would be supplied by my own energy. I would be entirely self-supporting, so to speak.

For about a month I rode about on my bicycle and was pleased as Punch with it. But one day when I was cycling along at full speed, a bus suddenly came out of a turning ahead of me. Half-dead with fear, I swerved from under its fire-breathing radiator, rode up on to the pavement and from there, with no reduction of speed, crashed into a watchmaker's shop.

"What's happened?!" shouted one of the watchmakers, jumping to his feet and dropping a Yerevan alarm clock, which rolled about the floor emitting a noise like an oriental tambourine.

"I shall claim repairs under the guarantee," I said in a calm voice, as I came to a sudden stop against the cash desk.

"He's a nut," the girl at the desk was the first to offer a solution, and slammed the pay window shut in a hurry.

I came to my senses and, so as not to dispel this favourable impression, silently wheeled my bicycle out of the shop. Out of the corner of my eye I noticed that one of

147

the watchmakers had let the magnifying glass drop out of his eye. For some reason it occurred to me that the watchmaker's magnifying glass and the aristocrat's monocle have a strange similarity of purpose. A watchmaker uses his glass to magnify tiny mechanisms while the man who wears a monocle probably thinks he is doing the same thing with people.

On the way home I was struck by the thought that while walking along beside a bicycle it is easier and safer to surrender oneself to one's dreams than while mounted on the saddle, and so I decided not to use my bicycle any more. After all, for a cyclist to compete with a bus is like a featherweight going into the ring with a heavyweight champion.

When I got home, I put my bicycle into the shed and forgot all about it.

About a month later a distant relative of mine paid us a visit and reminded me of it. In general, if a distant relative you haven't seen for a long time pays you a visit, you may expect no good to come of it. You have probably spent years of hard work establishing yourself while he has been gallivanting about God knows where. And then, when you have made your way in life and even acquired a bicycle of your own, he turns up bold as brass, grins at you with a whole mouthful of teeth and wants to start up a great family fellowship.

Imagine a stocky, thick-set man, in a fireproof leather jacket, with a rough powerful handshake. He has a job in town at a filling station and he lives in a village ten kilometres out of town. He is still a peasant and yet already a worker. He embodies in one person both the victorious classes.

And here in front of me stands this Vanechka Mamba, and such a store of vital energy bursts from every fold in his leather jacket, radiates from his lustrous eyes, from his firm, strong teeth, close-set as the bullet pouches down the front of a Circassian coat, that it seems he could quite easily drink a beer mug full of petrol and smoke a cigarette afterwards without doing himself any harm at all.

"Hullo there," he says, and grips my hand. The real rugged handshake of a man of great will power.

"Hullo," I say, "if it isn't Vanechka! Where have you been all this time?"

"I hear you want to sell a bike. I want to buy it."

I don't know what gave him the idea I wanted to sell my bicycle. I never suspected he knew of its existence. But Vanechka Mamba is one of those people who know more about you than you know about yourself. Still, why not sell it? I thought. It's a very good chance.

"Yes, it's up for sale," I said.

"How much?"

"Have a look at it first."

"I've had a look," he said, and grinned. "I noticed the shed was open."

The bike had cost about eight hundred in old money. I dropped a hundred for wear and tear.

"Seven hundred."

"No go."

"How much then?"

"Three hundred!"

Now we're going to strike a bargain, I thought. One of us will move up and the other will move down. At some point our interests must coincide.

"All right," I said, "six hundred."

"You're talking through your hat," he said. "Three hundred roubles don't grow on trees."

"But a bicycle does, of course?"

"Who rides a bicycle nowadays? Only the village postman."

"Why are you buying it then?"

"I have a long way to go to work. I just want it temporarily, till I buy a car."

"Going to buy a car and you haggle over the price of a bicycle."

"That's one reason why I'll be able to buy the car."

What was the use of arguing? That was Vanechka Mamba all over, quite a well-known character in our town, particularly among drivers.

"How much will you give me for it then?" I asked.

"What I said. You won't take it to market, will you?"

"No, I won't."

"And no second-hand shop would accept it either."

149

"All right, then," I said, "you can have it for four hundred, since you seem to know all about it."

"All right," said Vanechka, "I'll take it for three fifty, to make it fair all round. After all, we're related."

"To hell with you," I said. "Take it for three fifty. But how did you know I was selling my bicycle?"

"I saw the way you were riding it. That one won't be riding for long, I said to myself. Either he'll smash himself up or he'll sell it."

Vanechka cast a thrifty eye round the room and gave another smile with those bullet teeth of his.

"Got anything else to sell?"

"No," I said. "You've done well enough as it is."

We went out on to the porch. I stood on the steps and he went down into the yard and wheeled the bicycle out of the shed.

"Where's the pump?"

"Some kids pinched it."

"And you had the nerve to bargain!" Vanechka got on the bicycle and rode round the yard, lecturing me. "You'd better have a lock put on that shed. I'll bring you a good padlock."

"Never mind the lock," I said. "You give me the money."

"Next Sunday I'll sell my pears and bring it over." And he rode straight out of the yard without even getting off the bicycle.

I didn't like the look of that. But what could you do? After all he was my relative, though a very distant one. I've said it before and I'll say it again: one close friend is better than a dozen distant relatives. But this is not widely understood, particularly in our part of the world.

I met him in the street a week later.

"Well, have you sold your pears?"

"Yes, but you know how it is. The harvest was so good this year it would have been better to keep them for feeding the pigs."

"Didn't you make anything on them?"

"About enough to dress my womenfolk. You know yourself I've got five daughters. And my wife's pregnant again. They're ruining me, the bitches."

150

"Why torture your wife like this?" I said. "Give it a rest."

"I need a boy," he said. "As for the money, I won't let you down. The grapes will be ripe soon, then the persimmon, and after that the tangerines. I'll make ends meet somehow."

"Well, get on with it," I said.

And so we parted. You have to be considerate with people who owe you money. You have to pamper them. Sometimes you even have to spread a rumour about how honest and reliable they are.

The grape season came and went, then the persimmon and after that the tangerines, but Vanechka still did not appear.

Quite by chance I heard that his wife had again given birth to a girl and I decided to remind him of my existence by means of a congratulatory letter. You know the sort of thing. Congratulations on your new daughter. Come and see me some time. I'm still living in the same place. We'll sit together over a bottle of wine and have a chat.

The reply came a week later. What terrible handwriting you have, it said. My eldest daughter could hardly make it out. Thanks for the congratulations. My wife has given me another daughter. I'm properly mixed up now with the names. Now they have gone and installed electricity in our village. That means another thing to be paid for. But I have not forgotten my debt. Don't worry, Vanechka Mamba will get out of it somehow. And at the end of the letter he wanted to know whether I had bought a padlock yet for the shed. If I hadn't he would bring me one.

Well, I thought, that's goodbye to my money. I did not see him again till the following summer. By that time I had almost forgotten the debt.

I happened to be walking round the market one day when someone called out to me. I looked round and there was Vanechka Mamba, standing behind a mountain of water-melons. He had one great chunk in his mouth and was crunching it with his gleaming teeth.

"Mamba water-melons!" he was shouting. "Come and get 'em before I eat the lot myself!"

A woman asked me what kind of water-melon this was — the Mamba.

"Don't you know Mamba water-melons?" Vanechka exclaimed with a laugh and, spearing a succulent slice with his knife, pushed it under the woman's nose.

"I don't want to try it. I was just asking," the woman protested, turning away in embarrassment.

"I don't want you to buy it. All I'm asking is for you to taste a Mamba water-melon!" Vanechka almost sobbed.

In the end the woman had a taste and, once having had a taste, felt she had better not buy one. Every water-melon had a letter "M" carved on it, like a trade mark.

"What are these tagged atoms?" I said.

"An old chap and me, we brought these water-melons in from the village together. So I marked mine to make sure they didn't get mixed up."

He burst out laughing and, before I could remind him of his debt, pushed into my hands a weighty water-melon. I tried to refuse, but he admonished me sternly:

"We're relatives, aren't we? They're straight from our allotment. Home grown! Not from a shop!"

I had to take it. It's rather awkward to remind someone of a debt when you are holding a water-melon he has just given you, so I let it pass. To hell with it, I thought, at least I've got a water-melon in exchange for a bicycle.

Later I heard that he had swindled that old man properly. While they were riding to town perched on their water-melons in the back of the lorry, the old chap had dozed off and Vanechka with his pirate's knife had marked about twenty of the old man's melons with his own initial. So that's what a Mamba water-melon is!

Six months later I happened to call at a filling station with a friend of mine. My friend wanted some petrol for his car. And there was Vanechka busy hosing down a large Volga car, his face creased in an expression of sullen solicitude.

"Hullo, Vanechka," I said. "What are you now — a car washer?"

"Ah, hullo there," he said. He turned off his hose and came over to me. "Do you mean to say you haven't heard?"

"What should I have heard?"

"I've bought a Volga. This is my Volga."

"Good for you," I said. "You're a man of your word."

"And he calls himself a relative," Vanechka complained to my friend. "When he bought a bicycle I got to know about it at once. And yet when I buy a Volga he doesn't know a thing. It isn't fair, is it?"

"You'd better not mention that bicycle," I said.

"Why not?" he said. "I'll pay you for it, though it was a rotten old bike, with its pump missing too. But just at the moment I've started building a house and I'm up to my neck in debt. As soon as I've finished building I'll pay up all round."

"I suppose you use it to carry fruit?" I said.

"I should say I do. And it's ruining me! The traffic inspectors are crazy these days. Either they won't take a bribe at all or else they want so much it's not worth the journey."

When we had driven away, my friend said, "That Vanechka of yours is working a fiddle on petrol. He'll get caught."

"Let him," I said, although I was sure he would not be caught.

Some time later I met a mutual acquaintance.

"Have you heard? Vanechka Mamba's been taken to hospital in a very bad state."

"What happened?" I said. "Did the filling station blow up?"

"No," he said. "He fell into a lime pit. You knew he was building a house, didn't you?"

"Never mind," I said. "Vanechka will get out of it somehow."

"No, he won't. He's a gonner."

Vanechka was in hospital for about a month. I was going to visit him but felt awkward about it somehow. He might think I had come for my money. Then I heard he was up and about again. He had wriggled out of yet another tight corner. I had been quite sure he would. He had far too many dealings to occupy him in this world, and some of them were the kind you couldn't delegate to anyone else. No one else could have coped.

A year passed. One day I received an invitation to the

country. Vanechka had a double occasion to celebrate — his house-warming and the birth of a son.

I've seen enough of these celebrations. There are usually two or three hundred guests and they don't sit down to table till about midnight. What with all the preparations and waiting for the bosses to arrive. But the main thing is the presents. They have a village spokesman standing in the middle of the yard and a girl sitting at a table beside him, licking her pencil and writing down in an exercise book exactly who brings what. Some of the presents are in cash, but most of them are in kind.

"A vase, lovely as the moon," bawls the spokesman, holding it high above his head and displaying it to all the guests. "As pure and clear as the conscience of our dear guest," he adds inventively.

"A Russian eiderdown," he shouts, displaying the eiderdown with a flourish. "Big enough to cover a regiment," he comments brazenly, though the eiderdown is of quite ordinary size.

The people from the River Bzyb are outstanding in this respect. They can't open their mouths without exaggerating. While the master of ceremonies holds forth, the guest stands in front of him, his head bowed in comical modesty. Actually he is keeping an eye on the girl, to make sure she writes down his first and second names correctly. He then joins the onlookers and the master of ceremonies starts singing the praises of the next gift.

"A tablecloth fit for royalty," shouts this glibtongued individual and whirls the tablecloth into the air, as some rustic demon might whirl his cloak. In a word, it has to be seen to be believed. Of course, if you come without a present you won't be turned away, but a certain climate of opinion is created.

I didn't go. But I did send him a letter of congratulation, not hinting at anything.

One day I was standing in the station square of one of our smaller towns and wondering how best to get home. Should I take the train or try hitch-hiking?

I heard someone call my name, and there was Vanechka, poking his head out of his Volga.

"How did you get here?"

154

"Business. What about you?"

"Been on a trip to Sochi. Get in and I'll give you a lift."

I got in beside him and we started off. The air in the car was heavy with the persistent subtropical scent of illegally transported fruit. I had not seen Vanechka since his spell in hospital. He had scarcely changed at all, except that his face had lost a little of its colour, as though someone had dried it out with blotting paper. But he was still as cheerful as ever, with those gleaming teeth of his.

"I got your letter," he said. "We had a grand binge. Pity you didn't come."

"How did you manage to fall into that lime pit?"

"Oh, that? I'd rather not think about it. Nearly took off for the other world then. You can consider I've been there already. Still, it was thanks to that pit I got me a son."

"How so?"

"I reckon I didn't have enough lime in my body for a boy."

"You had plenty of lime all right."

"No, I mean it. Maybe I've made a scientific discovery. Write an article about it in one of your magazines and we'll go halves on the money. But they wouldn't print your stuff."

"Why not?" I asked guardedly.

"Your handwriting's no good. They wouldn't be able to read it."

"Why don't you stop ribbing me and tell me how you're getting on."

"Well, how shall I put it," he drawled, and with one hand flicked on the dashboard radio, picked up some jazz, tuned in and left it playing softly.

"There's no proper order anywhere," he declared suddenly. "That's what's wrong."

"What makes you so worried about order all of a sudden?"

"I've just been taking some tangerines to Sochi. Four inspectors in two hundred kilometres! Do you call that order? And don't interrupt," he added, though I had no intention of interrupting. "Three of them accept and the fourth refuses. Call that order? Can't they come to some agree-

155

ment between them! Either they accept or they don't, all of them. I can't tell him I've settled up with the other three, can I? That's dishonest, isn't it?"

"Of course, it is," I said, and I thought to myself what a funny thing this honesty is. Everyone cuts it down to suit his own needs, but the amazing thing is that no one can do without it.

"Now look here, Vanechka," I said. "You've got a car, you've got a house, you've got a son. Now give up this racket. What more do you want?"

"Hives," he said. "I want some hives."

"What kind of hives?"

"Bee-hives. My orchard's being sucked dry by other people's bees. I'd rather have some of my own. I want to give it a try."

"Try it by all means. You seem to have tried everything."

"Do you know of a good bee-keeper?"

"No, I don't."

We were silent for a while. But Vanechka is not the man to keep quiet, unless there's some hush money going.

"What's this campaign they've started about houses?"

"Why? Are they getting at you?"

"You know what a lot of envy there is about. People keep complaining. How did he get this house, this car... The chairman has had me up on the mat already."

"Well?"

"When a commission or a delegation comes round, I told him, you bring them to my place, don't you? Here's a well-to-do peasant, you say. And now you want to sell me down the river?"

"What did he say to that?"

"He said he had his own responsibilities to face.."

We never finished our conversation. Something quite unexpected happened.

We had been travelling fast but, despite the bends in our mountain roads, I felt I had nothing to worry about. Vanechka had done five years as a driver in the army and he had excellent road sense. We were just entering the town but he did not reduce speed. Suddenly a woman ran out of a bus queue opposite the station and bolted like a mad sheep across the road. Too late, I thought and even as the thought crossed my mind I heard the scream of brakes, the hiss of abrased rubber, the shouts of the crowd. The car hit the woman, knocked her to one side and stopped.

Some people ran up to the woman, picked her up and helped her off the road. Her face was pale and wooden. But all of a sudden she began to shake her fists and angrily push her helpers away.

A lad ran up to the car, glanced inside and bawled, "What are you waiting for, Vanechka? Step on it!"

Vanechka backed the car, drove round the station square, swung out on to the main road and put on such a turn of speed that the oncoming headlights flashed past us like meteors. We kept up this dizzy speed for about ten minutes and I was expecting at any moment that we should depart for a spot that Vanechka might perhaps wriggle out of but not I.

"Are you crazy," I shouted. "Slow down!"

I glanced round. A traffic inspector was chasing us on his motor-cycle. Vanechka swung into a side street and we went bouncing along a cobbled road. The motor-cycle disappeared for a moment only to reappear a few seconds later at the end of the block. Vanechka turned into a dark little alley, drove along it and jammed on his brakes so suddenly that I bumped my head on the door I had been clinging to. Two steps from the car yawned a freshly dug hole with a concrete pipe lying beside it. Vanechka tried to back out but went into a skid. The roar of the motor-cycle swelled menacingly in our ears, like fate itself.

A few seconds later the inspector pulled up beside us. He switched off his engine and came over with the springy tread of a lion-tamer.

"Why were you exceeding the speed limit? Why didn't you stop at once?"

"I didn't hear your signal, old man." It transpired that the inspector knew nothing of what had happened at the station. Nevertheless he was bent on getting something down in his notebook and kept asking Vanechka questions. Vanechka got out of the car. It was the first time I had seen him in such an abject state. He begged and pleaded, he swore by all his ancestors, he named mutual acquaintances, he argued that he and the inspector were really both part of the same system. Then I noticed him nodding significantly in my direction, obviously exaggerating the importance of my person. He made it look almost as though he were driving me on special instructions from the local government. I noticed myself assuming a rather dignified air.

In the end Vanechka talked the inspector round. He escorted him to his motor-cycle just as the local folk escort a man to his horse. I believe he would have held his stirrup if there had been one on the motor-cycle.

"Why, that fellow's just a beggar!" Vanechka declared unexpectedly, as soon as the traffic inspector had ridden away. It must have been a new inspector, one he had not yet got to know.

He climbed into the car and lit a cigarette. I decided that I had had enough adventures for one day and got out.

"Thanks," I said. "I haven't far to go now."

"Please yourself," he said and started the engine. "But what I told you about order was right."

"What kind of order?" I asked, baffled.

"They dug up this street, didn't they? Did they put up a sign? Did they show where the diversion was? Do you call that order?"

I spread my arms helplessly.

I could not leave before he had driven clear, so I waited. Vanechka put the car into reverse and, while it backed slowly, with skidding tyres along the street, I watched his resolute face with its harsh conquistador fold in the cheek clearly illuminated by the state electricity of a street lamp.

Yes, that was Vanechka — grasping, insolent, always boisterously cheerful. He was no fool, of course, but I would never advise anyone to take their water-melons to market with him.

After being in the car it was particularly pleasant to walk. I have a horror of road accidents, especially when pedestrians are involved. Thank goodness no blood was shed. The woman must have been frightened rather than hurt.

One day many years ago I was walking through Moscow

feeling in rather low spirits. I was just graduating from the institute and the faculty would not accept my diploma thesis. There was something about it they didn't like. It had frightened them somehow. Actually it was rather a silly piece of work, but the heads of the faculty, and I myself for that matter, were slow to realise this. Later on, when I had to defend it, its foolishness was safely exposed and I got a good mark for it. But that day in the street I was depressed. It was cold and slippery and there was wet ice on the pavements. Suddenly I noticed a lorry backing out of a narrow passage between two buildings. There were two little boys on the pavement, one about eight, the other nearer four. At the sight of the approaching lorry the elder boy abandoned the little one and ran to safety. I shouted at the top of my voice. The little fellow heard nothing. He was watching the pigeons and had lapsed into that state of profound meditation that is known only to philosophers and children. He was so small that the end of the lorry had already passed unhindered over his head. I managed to run up and drag him away in time. Luckily the lorry had been moving very slowly, the driver being particularly careful because of the ice.

The little boy never realised what had happened. He was warmly wrapped up and only his fresh little face was visible under a fur hat with earflaps. Neither mothers nor drivers are proof against all eventualities, and this is where the pedestrians come in. And even they derive some benefit from such incidents. At that moment I made up my mind once and for all that the meaning of life did not lie in diploma work, nor even in the opinion of the faculty, but in something else.

Perhaps, in being a decent kind of pedestrian? At bottom, all these cars, aeroplanes, locomotives are really nothing but the children's perambulators that we pedestrians either pull or push.

After sitting for so long in someone else's car it was a pleasant relief to be walking on firm ground. The earth is always ours, no matter who or what makes it spin. The main thing is the sense of freedom and peace it gives us. You are not being moved by some external force, you are moving yourself. And what's more, you cannot run anybody over. Of course, someone may run you over, but then you could also be hit on the head by a falling brick. The main thing is not to throw bricks about.

I walked home congratulating myself on never having bought a car, and on having sold my bicycle.

I think our best thoughts occur to us when we are moving at a speed of not more than five kilometres per hour.

ONE DAY IN SUMMER

One hot summer day I was sitting near the pier eating ice-cream sprinkled with broken nuts. That's the kind of ice-cream they sell here. First they put firm little dollops in a metal dish, then sprinkle nuts on top. I suppose I could have refused the nuts (peanuts, to be exact), but no one else did, so I didn't either.

The girl at the ice-cream counter in her crisp white overall, looking cool and therefore pleasant, was working silently, in a smooth, steady rhythm. No one wanted to break this established rhythm. It was too hot and we were all too lazy.

The flowering oleanders cast light shadows on the tables of the open-air café. A salutary breeze from the sea drifted through their straggling branches carrying a sweetish smell of decay from the tired pink flowers. Through the oleanders I could see the pier and the sea.

Now and then anglers' boats would pass slowly each with its home-made trawl consisting of a basket on an iron hoop.

It was Saturday and they were catching shrimps in preparation for the morrow's fishing. Sometimes a boat would heave to and the men in the stern would haul in the basket with its heavy load of sand and silt and bend over it, searching for the shrimps and slopping handfuls of silt over the side. Having emptied the basket, they would rinse it out, then throw it over the stern again and row as far away from it as possible so as not to frighten the shrimps with their boat. They were keeping very close to the shore because in this kind of weather shrimps come right up to the water's edge.

On the upper deck of the pier holiday-makers were queueing for the launch. From the water came the sound of boys' voices vying with each other in asking, or rather, demanding that the people in the queue should throw them coins. Responding reluctantly to these urgings, someone would occasionally toss a coin into the water. Judging by the faces that peered over the rail, this occupation afforded no one any great amusement. One of the lads stayed at some distance from the pier and kept demanding throws into the deep water. Sometimes a sparkling coin would fly in his direction. It was harder for him to catch it out there, of course, but on the other hand he had no rivals to contend with and could work in peace.

Some of the lads were diving straight off the pier. The sound of their bodies splashing into the water and of their young voices was refreshing. When a launch arrived and took on its passengers, the lads who had been lucky enough to retrieve a few coins ran up the steps and bought ice-cream. Wet and shivering, they would devour their portions with a noisy clattering of spoons, then run back to the pier.

"Is this seat free?" I heard a man's voice above my head.

Beside me stood a man holding a dish of ice-cream and a folded newspaper.

"Yes," I said.

He nodded, drew back a chair and sat down. I had been so taken up with the sea that I had failed to notice his approach. His accent and a slight drawl told me that he was a German. He was in his mid-fifties, sunburnt, with a vigorous crop of short fair hair, a slightly asymmetrical face and bright, clear eyes.

The newspaper was one of our Black Sea publications. He scanned it for a while, laid it aside with a little smirk and set about his ice-cream. The smirk emphasised the lopsidedness of his face and I wondered if the habit of smirking in this fashion had perhaps pulled the lower part of his otherwise regular features to one side.

Curious to know what it was he had laughed at, I tried to peep into his newspaper.

"Want to read it?" he asked promptly, noticing my not very skilful attempt, and held it out to me.

"No," I said and, sensing in his tone a desire for communication, added, "You speak very good Russian."

"Yes, I do," he assented, and his bright eyes flashed

even brighter. "And I'm proud of it. Still, I've been studying the language since I was a boy."

"Have you really?" I said.

"Yes," he repeated vigorously, and added with an unexpected touch of slyness, "Can you guess why?"

"I don't know," I said, trying not to look quite so sociable, if that was what my face had expressed in the first place. "To be able to read Dostoyevsky in the original?"

"Exactly," he nodded, and pushed aside the empty ice-cream dish. All this time he had been hard at work on its contents without for a moment letting me out of range of his intensely bright eyes. To perform both these tasks at once he had been forced to lower at me most of the time.

"How do you find it here?" I asked.

"Good," he nodded again. "I came with my wife and daughter, though it's very expensive here."

"Where are they?" I asked.

"I'm waiting for them to come back from the beach," he said, and looked at his watch. "I decided to go for a walk in town by myself today."

"Look here," I said suddenly, trying not to appear too enthusiastic. "Suppose we drink a bottle of champagne together?"

"I'm with you," he said good-naturedly, and spread his arms.

I rose and went to the bar. All blue plastic and glass, with dazzling streamlined curves, the bar looked more like a flying machine than part of a catering establishment.

Surrounded by this synthetic splendour sat the bartender eating hominy and cheese in an attitude of bucolic bliss. His wife was standing over him and at his knee, with one hand rummaging thoughtfully in a large drawerful of sweets, was a child.

"Champagne and a kilo of apples," I said, having inspected the counter.

The one and only waitress was standing next to me, her back against the bar, eating ice-cream. The barman wiped his hands with a rag and, clicking his tongue, reached into the ice-barrel. The waitress did not stir.

163

11*

"He's a foreigner," I said with a nod in the direction of my table.

The barman responded with a comprehending motion of the head and I sensed his hand going deeper among the tinkling icicles in the barrel. The waitress went on calmly eating her ice-cream.

"Tell the kids to keep quiet," I heard the barman's voice behind me.

The young coin-divers had taken over a free table next to ours. Their elbows were beating a tattoo on the table. One of them kept shaking his head to get the water out of his ear, and this sent the others into fits of irrestrainable laughter. Their wet, sunburnt skin was speckled with goose pimples. They all looked the picture of health, and it was pleasant to watch them.

The waitress brought a dish of apples and a bottle of champagne. Having put the dish on the table, she started taking the foil off the bottle. The lads at the next table froze in expectation of the pop, but then I noticed that the waitress had forgotten the glasses and stopped her. Not in the least offended by my interference, nor in any way embarrassed by her own mistake, she went for the glasses. She appeared to have a very keen sense of her own independence, and also to take a secretly ironic view of her customers. It was particularly noticeable as she walked away swinging her broad hips, but not too much, just for her own pleasure, not for anyone else's benefit.

A minute later she reappeared with two tall narrow glasses. She removed the cork skilfully, letting out the air little by little, so that the boys, who had again frozen in expectation of a big bang, were once again disappointed. We drank to having made each other's acquaintance.

"Magnificent stuff," said the German, and replaced his empty glass firmly on the table. Tiny beads of perspiration had broken out on his forehead. The champagne really was good.

"Were you living in Germany during the time of the nazis?" I asked when the conversation turned to Mikhail Romm's film *Ordinary Fascism*, which he praised highly. Apparently he had seen it at home in West Germany.

"Yes," he said. "From start to finish."

"Well, it's all over now," I said. "What do you think? Was Hitler a clever or gifted man in his way?"

"He was never a clever man," the German shook his head, twisting his lip a little to one side. "But he did possess some sort of hypnotic gift, I believe."

"In what sense?"

"His speeches roused the mob, worked them up into a kind of politico-sexual psychosis."

"What about *Mein Kampf?*" I said. "What would you call that?"

"In form it's typical stream of consciousness. But in contrast to Joyce, it's a stream of very foolish consciousness."

"Never mind the form," I said. "The thing that interests me is how he set about proving, let us say, the necessity for exterminating the Slavs."

"In *Mein Kampf* that was all wrapped up in very vague phrases. It was only brought out into the open after they had got power. *Mein Kampf* was written in 1924. On the whole, it's a wretched, semi-literate piece of work," he added contemptuously, and I felt that the subject had begun to bore him.

"Is that what you think now or have you always thought so?" I asked.

"Always," he replied, rather haughtily it seemed to me, and added suddenly, "and I nearly paid the price for it."

He paused as if to recall something or, perhaps, wondering whether to continue.

"Are you tired of my questions?" I asked, pouring champagne.

"Not a bit," he replied promptly, and having sipped at his glass again, set it down firmly on the table. Apparently he had some doubts about the stability of the glass.

"It was just a boys' prank," he said with a smile. "Two of my friends and I got into our university one night and scattered pamphlets around. We quoted a few illiterate passages from *Mein Kampf* and argued that a man who didn't know the German language properly could not claim to be leader of the German people."

"And what happened?" I asked, trying not to appear too curious.

"We were saved by the primitive mentality of the police," he said and rose, emptying his glass, at the sound of the launch's siren.

"I'll be back in a moment," he said with a nod, and set off briskly towards the pier, moving fast on his muscular legs.

I noticed that he was wearing shorts.

The boys' table was now occupied by a local pensioner, a smallish chubby old man in a clean tussore tunic. On the table before him stood a bottle of Borzhomi mineral water and a small tumbler, from which he would occasionally take two or three sips, then munch his lips and, fingering a string of prayer beads, go on watching the passers-by with idle curiosity.

Everything about him seemed to say: here am I, I've worked hard all my life and now I'm enjoying a well-earned rest. I drink Borzhomi if I want to, I count my beads if I want to, and, if I want to, I can just sit and look at you. And there's nothing to stop you doing a good job of work in life so that afterwards, when your time comes, you too can enjoy a well-earned rest as I am doing now.

At first he was alone, then he was joined by a big carelessly made-up woman wearing a necklace of wooden beads, who sat down at his table with a dish of ice-cream. They talked animatedly and all the time the old man's voice seemed to emanate à chilly intellectual superiority, which his companion sought ineffectually to melt, with the result that her own voice began to betray a certain secret resentment and even reproach. But this the old man ignored, persisting obstinately in the tone he had adopted from the start. I listened.

"Japan is now considered a great country," the pensioner remarked. "And as a matter of fact they do have some very beautiful women."

"But the men are all ugly," his companion retorted joyfully. "In 'forty-five I saw lots of Japanese POWs in Irkutsk and there wasn't a single good-looking man among them."

"Prisoners of war are never good-looking," the pensioner interrupted superciliously, as though revealing some profound psychological truth behind her ethnographical observation and thus disposing of the modest value of the observation itself.

"I don't see why..." the woman began, but the old man in tussore silk raised his finger and she fell silent.

"However, Japan is at the same time a major source of potential aggression," he said, "because she is tied up with America through banking capital."

"If you ask me, they're all a lot of scoundrels in America, except for about ten per cent," the woman responded and, noticing the old man touching his beads, herself began to finger her necklace.

"A country of enormous wealth," the pensioner proclaimed thoughtfully, and propped his elbows on the table, two sharp, uncompromising elbows outlined through the wide sleeves of his tussore tunic.

"Dupont's daughter," he began, but the thought of the educational level of his audience made him pause, "Do you know who Dupont is?"

The woman looked confused. "Oh yes, that one..."

"Dupont is a multi-millionaire," the old man declared harshly. "And compared with a multi-millionaire a millionaire is considered a mere beggar."

"Good heavens," the woman sighed.

"Well," the pensioner continued, "Dupont's daughter came to a reception wearing diamonds worth ten million dollars. Now I suppose you'll ask why no one robbed her?"

The old man leaned back, as though offering time and space for the widest conjecture.

"Why?" the woman asked, still overawed by the wealth of the multi-millionaires.

"Because she was guarded by fifty detectives disguised as distinguished foreign guests," the pensioner concluded triumphantly, and sipped at his Borzhomi from the small tumbler.

"Now they've published Admiral Nelson's private correspondence," the woman remarked. "A man can write all sorts of things to a woman..."

"I know," the old man interrupted sternly. "But that's the English."

"It's a shame anyhow," said the woman.

167

"Vivien Leigh," the pensioner continued, "tried to save the admiral's honour but she failed."

"I know," said the woman, "she's dead, isn't she?"

"Yes," the old man affirmed. "She died of tuberculosis because she wasn't allowed to have any sex life. When a person has tuberculosis or cancer," holding the beads in one hand he bent down two fingers on the other, "all sex life is categorically forbidden!"

This sounded like some kind of mild warning. The old man glanced sideways at the woman, trying to sense her attitude to the matter.

"I know," the woman said, not allowing him to sense anything.

"Vissarion Belinsky also died of tuberculosis," the old man recalled suddenly.

"Tolstoy is my favourite writer."

"It depends which Tolstoy," he corrected her. "There were three of them."

"Leo Tolstoy, of course," she replied.

"*Anna Karenina*," he remarked, "is the greatest family novel of all times and all nations."

"But why was she so jealous in her love of Vronsky?!" the woman exclaimed, as if she had been sorrowing over this for years. "That's such a terrible thing. Quite unendurable."

A crowd of holiday-makers had left the beach and was drifting lazily up the street. The foreign women among them in their short beach robes seemed particularly long-legged. A few years ago they had not been allowed to walk into town in such attire; now apparently it was tolerated. My new acquaintance reappeared.

"They seem to be very late," he said without any special regret

I poured out some more champagne.

"That's German punctuality for you," I said.

"German punctuality is very much exaggerated," he replied.

We drank. He took an apple from the dish and bit into it vigorously.

"So it was the primitive mentality of the police that

168

saved you?" I reminded him when he had swallowcd his bite of apple.

"Yes," he nodded, and went on, "the Gestapo turned the whole philosophical faculty upside down but for some reason they left us alone. They decided it must have been the work of students whose line of study would enable them to compare Hegel's style with Hitler's. One day all the students of the philosophical faculty had their lecture notes confiscated, although we had printed our pamphlets in block capitals. Two of the students refused to surrender their notes and were taken straight from the university to the Gestapo."

"What did they do to them?" I asked.

"Nothing," he replied, allowing his asymmetrical face to break into a sardonic smile. "Released them the next day with profound apologies. These brave fellows had influence in high places. One of them had an uncle who worked in Goebbels' office, or pretty near it. Admittedly, while they were finding this out, they gave him a nice..." He paused and made an eloquent gesture with his fist.

"Black-eye," I suggested.

"Yes, a black-eye," he repeated the expression that had evaded him with some pleasure. "And he went about for a whole week with that black-eye, very proud of it. Actually that was one of the typical things about the Reich — a return to primitive tribal relationships."

"Was this deliberate or part of the logic of the regime?"

"Both, I think," he replied after a pause. "The Reich bosses tried to pick their men on a local as well as a family basis. Sharing the same accent, the same memories of a certain part of the country and so on provided them with a substitute for what educated people call spiritual affinity. And then, of course, there was the system of the invisible hostage. Our family, for instance, lived in constant fear because of mother's brother. He had been a Social-Democrat, arrested in 'thirty-four. For several years we were able to correspond with him, then our letters started coming back stamped 'adressat unbekannt', meaning that the person they were addressed to was no longer there. We told mother he must have been moved to another camp where correspondence was not allowed, but my father and

I suspected that he had been killed. And after the war we learned that he had been."

"Tell me," I said, "wasn't this a handicap for you while you were at college or at work?"

"Not directly," he said slowly, speaking between pauses, "but one always had a feeling of uncertainty or even guilt. It's a difficult kind of feeling to express in words. You have to experience it in reality. It seemed to get stronger, then tail off, then come on again. But it never disappeared altogether. A kind of inferiority complex towards the state—that's how I would define that particular condition."

"You put it very clearly," I said and poured out the rest of the champagne. Whether it was the drink or the precision of his definition I am not sure, but I did envisage very clearly the condition he had described.

"To give you an even better idea, I'll tell you about something that happened to myself," he said and, smacking his lips, placed his empty glass on the table. He was certainly enjoying the champagne.

"What about another bottle?" I suggested.

"Fine," he said, "but you must let me pay for it."

"That would be contrary to our custom," I said, swelling with pride in my own generosity.

I held up the empty bottle for the waitress to see. She was watching a workman crouched beside the barrel where the ice-cream was kept. He was breaking up a large lump of ice wrapped in wet sackcloth. The waitress nodded and turned unwillingly to the bar. My companion offered me a cigarette and lit one himself.

The pensioner was still talking to the woman at his table. I listened again.

"Churchill," he declared sententiously, "recognised no other drink except Armenian brandy and Georgian Borzhomi."

"Wasn't he afraid they'd take their revenge on him?" said the woman, nodding at the bottle of Borzhomi.

"No," the pensioner replied blandly. "Stalin had promised him. And you know how Stalin kept his word?"

"Of course," said the woman.

"I wonder," the German remarked, "what is the popular local wine here?"

"I have read the Stalin-Churchill correspondence," the pensioner said. "It's an extremely rare book."

"At the moment," I said, still listening to the conversation at the next table, "*Isabella* is the favourite."

"You couldn't lend it to me to read, could you?" the woman asked.

"Never heard of it," said my companion after some reflection.

"No, I cannot, my dear," the pensioner replied more gently, to soften the refusal. "But I can let you have some other rare book. I've been collecting rare books ever since I retired."

"It's a local peasant wine," I said. "It happens to be in fashion at the moment."

The German nodded.

"Have you got *Woman in White?*"

"Of course," the pensioner nodded. "I have all the rare books."

"Lend it to me. I read fast," she said.

"I can't lend you *Woman in White*, but you can have any of my other rare books."

"But why can't you lend me *Woman in White?*" she asked bitterly.

"Not because I don't trust you but because someone else has it at present," said the old man.

"Fashion is a remarkable thing," my companion observed suddenly, stubbing out his cigarette on the side of the ash-tray. "In the 'twenties there used to be a popular film actor who made himself up to look exactly like Hitler."

"How do you mean?"

"He either sensed or foresaw the kind of looks that would appeal to the lower middle classes as a whole. And a few years later the image he had created turned up in the real person of Adolph Hitler."

"That's very interesting," I said.

The waitress came up with a fresh bottle of champagne. Instead of allowing her to uncork it, I took the cool wet bottle myself. She cleared away the empty ice-cream dishes.

I removed the foil from the neck of the bottle and,

holding down the white plastic cork with one hand, unfastened the wire with the other. The cork pressed up against my hand with all the force of a strong, living creature. I released the air gradually, then poured out the champagne. As I tipped the bottle a wisp of vapour rose from the neck.

We each drank a full glass. The new bottle was even cooler and tasted better still.

"After I had graduated," he said, still replacing his glass on the table in the same firm, deliberate manner, "I was accepted by the institute of the famous Professor Hartz. In those days I was considered a young and promising physicist and they put me in a group engaged in theoretical studies. The scientists at our institute led a rather secluded existence and tried to cut themselves off as much as possible from the life around them. But this was becoming more and more difficult, if only because one might easily be killed any day by the American bombing. In 1943 several districts in our town were bombed so badly that even the medieval enthusiasts could not pass them off as picturesque ruins. More and more cripples from the Eastern Front kept appearing in the town, and more and more tormented women's and children's faces, but Goebbels' propaganda went on proclaiming victory, in which by this time no one, in our circle at least, had any belief whatever.

"One Sunday afternoon, when I was sitting in my room reading a novel of pre-nazi days, I heard the voices of my wife and someone else, a man, coming from the next room. My wife's voice sounded worried. She opened the door and looked anxiously into my room.

" 'There's someone to see you,' she said, and stood aside to admit a person who was a complete stranger to me.

" 'You're wanted at the institute,' he said after a brief greeting. 'It's for an urgent conference.'

" 'Why didn't they ring me up?' I asked, watching him closely. He must be some new man from the administrative side, I decided.

" 'You can probably guess,' he said significantly.

" 'But why on Sunday?' my wife protested.

172

" 'We don't discuss orders from our superiors,' he retorted with a shrug.

"By that time we were used to the police making a great show of vigilance around our institute. There was nothing we could do about it. You had only to ring from one room to another to speak to a colleague about some problem connected with our work and the line would go dead. This was regarded as a means of protecting us against any leakage of information. Now, apparently, they had decided to inform us of top-secret conferences by their own official messengers.

" 'I'll be ready in a minute,' I said, and began changing.

" 'Perhaps you would like a cup of coffee?' my wife suggested. I could still feel the alarm in her voice.

" 'Very well,' I replied, and nodded to reassure her.

" 'Thank you,' the man said, and sat down in an armchair, glancing out of the corner of his eye at the bookshelves. My wife left the room.

" 'I am from the Gestapo,' the man informed me when he had heard the door close behind my wife in the next room. He said this in a toneless voice as if trying to contain the explosive force of his statement as far as possible.

"I felt my fingers instantly go numb and fumbled helplessly to button my shirt. By a great effort of will I managed to overcome their rigidity and guide the buttons into place, and then adjust my neck-tie. To this day I remember those few seconds of suffocating silence, the deafening rustle of my starched shirt, the sudden irritation with my wife for always using just that little bit too much starch in the washing and — most surprising of all! — the sense of embarrassment at having to do something so disrespectful as change my clothes in this stranger's presence, while all the time the underlying thought behind these sensations was that I must not hurry, must not show any sign of alarm.

" 'Well, what can I do for you?' I asked him at last.

" 'I am sure it's something quite trivial,' he said without the slightest expression in his voice, apparently still listening for any sounds in the other room. The sound of a door opening told us that my wife was bringing the coffee.

"We looked at each other and he understood my silent inquiry at once.

"'No need to cause anxiety,' he said, and gave me a significant glance. I nodded as cheerfully as I could. I had to show that I had nothing to be afraid of and was confident of getting home soon. I slipped a marker into the novel I had been reading, closed it briskly and dropped it on the table. If he had been watching my behaviour, this gesture should have told him that I expected to return to my book that evening.

"'We have decided we had better go rightaway,' he said rising, when my wife appeared in the doorway with a steaming tray.

"'It can't be as urgent as all that,' I protested.

"I took a cup of coffee and drank it standing, in a few searing gulps. He also sipped a little coffee. My wife was still disturbed. She realised that while she had been out of the room I must have elicited some more definite information from my visitor and she looked inquiringly into my eyes. I gave no answer to her glance. She looked at him but he remained even more inscrutable. There was something indefinably odd about him. Perhaps it was the oddiness of the insurance agent. His dark-blue mackintosh gave him a rather sombre elegance.

"'But you'll be back for dinner?' she asked, when I had returned the cup to the tray. It was still four hours till dinner time.

"'Of course,' I said, and looked at him. He nodded, either to confirm what I had said or in approval of my taking up his game.

"When we had left and the house was some distance behind us, he halted and said, 'I'll go on ahead and you'll follow.'

"'At what distance?' I asked, marvelling at my own readiness to live according to their instructions.

"'About twenty paces,' he said, 'I'll wait for you at the entrance.'"

"'All right,' I said, and he walked on ahead of me. There were two weak spots in my biography — the fate of my uncle and the pamphlets. I realised they must know all about my uncle. But how much did they know about the pamphlets? Six years had passed since then. But for them there was no statue of limitations and they never forgave anything. Surely none of the others had let it out? I had told only one other person, an old school-friend of mine. I trusted him as much as I trusted myself. But perhaps one of the others had, like myself, confided in a friend and that friend had betrayed him? But if they knew something, why did they not arrest me straightaway? Turning all this over in my mind, I walked on in the wake of my escort. He seemed to be in no hurry. In his slouch hat and dark-blue mackintosh he now looked more like a street lounger.

"The Gestapo office was situated in an old mansion surrounded by tall plane trees. On one side it looked over a field, where some schoolboys were playing football. Several bicycles lay gleaming in the grass. It was strange to see these lads and hear their excited voices so near this sinister building whose purpose was common knowledge in the town. The pavement on this side of the street was almost deserted. People preferred to keep to the other side. I followed my escort down a dimly lit corridor. There was no guard at the door. My escort stopped and waited for me at a pass-office window. When he saw me approaching, he caught the duty officer's eye and nodded in my direction. The duty officer was speaking on the phone. He glanced at me and put down the receiver.

"There was a cup of tea on his desk with a crushed slice of lemon floating in it. He stirred it with a spoon and sipped. We walked on down the corridor, at the end of which I could make out the iron cage of a lift. We entered the lift. He slammed the iron door and pressed a button. The lift stopped on the third floor.

"We came out of the lift and walked down a long corridor lit by dim electric bulbs, then turned down a side corridor and into another and at last, when I thought the corridors would never end, we halted at a door padded with black leather, or some kind of material that looked like black leather.

"My escort nodded to me to wait, took off his hat and opened the door a little. But even before he opened it, he and his dark-blue mackintosh seemed to melt into the black background of the door. This corridor like all the others was poorly lighted.

"Five minutes later the door opened again and I saw the pale blob of my escort's face in the blackness of the door. The blob nodded and I entered the room.

"It was a large, well lighted room with windows looking out over the field where the boys were still playing football. I had not expected to find myself on this side of the building. It may have been pure coincidence but at the time I was sure they had deliberately confused my sense of direction. The large desk was bare save for an inkstand, an open folder and a pile of clean notepaper. Behind it sat a man of about thirty with a narrow, carefully shaven face. We greeted each other and he extended his hand to me over the desk.

"'Won't you sit down,' he said, and nodded to an armchair. I sat down. He spent a minute or so rather casually leafing through the contents of the file that lay in front of him. The desk was very wide and it was quite impossible to read what he was looking at. But I was certain that the file was about me.

"'Have you been at the institute long?' he asked, still thumbing the pages casually. I replied briefly, quite sure that he knew far more about me than his question indicated. He turned a few more pages.

"'In what department?' he asked. I named my department and he nodded, still examining the file as though seeking confirmation of what I had told him.

"'How do they feel at the institute about the war against Russia?' he asked, and this time he raised his head.

"'Like the whole German people,' I said.

"A faint expression of boredom appeared in his dark, almond-shaped eyes.

"'Could you be more specific?'

"'Scientists are not very interested in politics, you know,' I said.

"'Unfortunately,' he nodded pompously and, putting

176

on a more dignified air, added suddenly. 'Do you know that the Führer himself finds time to take an interest in the work of your institute?'

"A glassy look came into his eyes and for a second his whole appearance bore a distant resemblance to Hitler.

"'Yes, I do,' I said.

"The institute authorities had often told us confidentially about this and made it clear that in response to this exceptional interest on the part of the Führer we should display exceptional zeal in our work.

"'But the Führer is not the only person who is interested in your work,' he continued after a generous pause, in which I was granted time to enjoy the pleasant side of the matter. 'The enemies of the Reich are also interested.'

"The glassy look reappeared in his eyes and he again resembled the Führer, this time in expressing ruthlessness towards the Reich's enemies.

"I shrugged. This was a relief. Apparently he did not know about my escapade at the university. He went back to the file, leafed through it, then stopped suddenly and began to read a page with raised eyebrows. The tension grew inside me again. He did know, after all.

"'Your uncle seems to have been a Social-Democrat?' he queried, as though he had quite by chance discovered a slight blemish in my intellectual background. Even the way he said 'your uncle' seemed to express contempt for, rather than hatred of, the Social-Democrats.

"'Yes, he is,' I said.

"'Where is he now?' he asked, making no attempt to conceal the falsity in his voice. I told him the whole story, which he knew perfectly well already.

"'There you are, you see,' he nodded, and his tone seemed to indicate that this was the inevitable outcome of such hopelessly obsolete patriarchal convictions. But I was wrong. His tone indicated something quite different.

"'There you are,' he repeated. 'We trust you, but what is your response?'

"'I trust you too,' I said, as firmly as I could.

177

"He nodded. 'Yes, I know you are a patriot, even though your uncle was a Social-Democrat.'

"'Was?' I could not help repeating, and felt a sudden stab of pain in the chest. We had kept hope alive in spite of everything. Apparently the Gestapo man had said more than he intended. Or was he merely pretending to have done so?

"'Was and still is,' he corrected himself, but this sounded even more hopeless. 'I know you are a patriot,' he repeated, 'but the time has come for you to show your patriotism in practice.'

"'What have you in mind?' I asked. The hand leafing through the file stopped for a moment and appeared to stroke an unopened page. He seemed scarcely able to resist the pleasure of turning it. Once again I had a suspicion that he knew something about those pamphlets.

"'Help us in our work,' he said simply, and looked into my eyes.

"I had never expected this. My face must have expressed either fright or revulsion.

"'You won't have to come here,' he added quickly. 'One of our people will meet you about once a month and you will tell him...'

"'Tell him what?' I interrupted.

"'The attitude of scientists, instances of hostile or subversive statements,' he said evenly. 'We need relevant information, not surveillance. You know how much importance is attached to your institute.'

"He sounded like a doctor persuading a patient to take the prescribed medicines.

"His dark, almond-shaped eyes were watching me steadily. The skin on his clean-shaven, bluish face was so taut that it looked as if any grimace, any private expression would cause him pain by pinching the already overstrained skin. He therefore tried to maintain only one expression on his face that was in line with the general direction of his service.

"'If it were a matter of any hostile statements,' I said, involuntarily bringing my own voice and face in line with this general direction, 'I would consider it my duty to bring them to your notice in any case.'

178

"As soon as I began to say this the faint expression of boredom again appeared in his eyes and I suddenly realised that all this was to him merely a long familiar form of refusal.

"'Bearing in mind the fact that we are at war,' I added, to make it sound more convincing. This had eased the situation. It was not the first time they had heard a refusal.

"'Yes, of course,' he said expressionlessly, and reached out for the telephone as it began to ring.

"'Yes,' he said, and a voice grated in the receiver. 'Yes,' he repeated from time to time as the voice went on. His monosyllabic replies sounded impressive and I sensed that he was playing the high official for my benefit.

"'He's bluffing,' he said suddenly into the receiver, and I gave an involuntary start. 'Here, in my room,' he added. 'Come over.'

"All this time he must have been talking about me over the phone. This fisher of my soul now rose to his feet, took a bundle of keys out of his pocket and walked over to a safe and, as he did so, another man entered the room. I felt instinctively that this must be the person who had just been speaking on the phone. He glanced at me with a kind of casual curiosity, and I decided that they had not been talking about me.

"The first Gestapo man opened his safe and bent forward to look inside. I caught a glimpse of several rows of mousy-coloured files standing tightly packed on the shelves. He hooked two fingers into one of them and prised it out. The file actually seemed to resist and at the last moment, as it reluctantly gave in, emitted a kind of squeal, like the cry of a captured animal.

"The files were so tightly packed that the row closed again at once, as though nothing had been removed. The other man took the file and silently left the room.

"'So you don't want to co-operate with us?' said my interrogator, resuming his seat. His hand again glided to the unopened page and stroked it.

"'Hardly that,' I said, feeling my eyes drawn irresistibly to the page that was quivering under his hand.

179

"'Or is it your uncle's principles that forbid it?' he asked. I felt the spring of annoyance within him begin to tighten. And all of a sudden I realised that the main thing now was not to show him that it was normal human decency that prevented me from having any connection with him.

"'Principles have nothing to do with it,' I said. 'It's simply that every job demands a sense of vocation.'

"'You should try. Perhaps you have the right one,' he said. The spring had slackened a little.

"'No,' I said, after a little reflection. 'I am no good at hiding my thoughts. I am far too talkative.'

"'Is that a hereditary defect?'

"'No,' I said, 'just part of my character.'

"'By the way, what was this incident at the university?' he asked suddenly, raising his head. I had not noticed him turn the page.

"'What incident?' I asked, feeling a dryness in my throat.

"'Shall I remind you?' he asked, pointing to the page.

"'I don't remember any incident,' I said, and braced myself.

"We eyed each other for several long seconds. If he knows, I thought, I have nothing to lose. And if he doesn't know, this is still the only way to act.

"'Very well,' he said suddenly, drawing a clean sheet from the pile of paper and placing it before me. 'Put it all down on paper.'

"'Put what down?'

"'That you refuse to help the Reich,' he said.

"So he doesn't know, I thought, feeling renewed strength. He knows that there was some such incident while I was studying but nothing more. And now I took a quiet pleasure in estimating the extent of his knowledge.

"'I'm not refusing,' I said, pushing the sheet gently aside.

"'So you agree, then?'

"'I am quite prepared to carry out my duty to my country, but without these formalities,' I said, trying to choose the mildest possible expressions. The pamphlet danger seemed to have passed, but I was afraid he might bring

it up again. At the moment when he had asked me
straight out, I had been almost certain that he had no
precise knowledge, but now that the danger seemed to
have passed I was even more afraid to return to this
dark spot. Instinctively I was trying to get as far away
from it as possible and I sensed that this could only be
done at the price of some concession. He can only be
diverted by the chance of a breakthrough somewhere
else, I thought.

"'No,' he said, and a rather sentimental note crept
into his voice, 'you'd better put it down honestly in black
and white that you refuse to perform your patriotic
duty.'

"'I'll think it over,' I said.

"'Yes, of course you must,' he said amicably and,
opening a drawer, took out a cigarette and lighted it.
'Have a smoke?' he suggested.

"'Yes,' I said.

"He produced an open packet from his drawer and
offered it to me. I took a cigarette, and then noticed
that his own cigarette was from another, more expensive
packet. I almost laughed in his face as he offered me
a light. Even in this, apparently, he had to feel his superiority.

"I was silent and so was he. I was supposed to be
thinking things over. Silence was to my advantage.

"'You should bear in mind', he recalled suddenly,
'that our service has not done away with material in-
centives.'

"'In what sense?' I asked. This was subject worth
developing. I had to impress upon him that I was moving
in his direction.

"'We don't pay too badly,' he said.

"'How much?' I asked with deliberate arrogance.
I had to show him that he had succeeded in overcoming
what they would call my weak-kneed intellectual scruples.
A flicker of resentment appeared in his eyes — this was
an insult to the firm. Perhaps I had gone too far.

"'That would depend on the fruitfulness of your
work,' he said. Yes, fruitfulness — that was the word he
used.

"I shook my head regretfully, as if I had been considering my budget. 'No,' I said. 'They don't pay me too badly at the institute.'

"'But in time we shall be able to provide you with a good flat,' he said in some alarm. Now we were bargaining.

"'I have a good flat already,' I said.

"'We'll give you a flat in a district that has the best air-raid shelter in the city,' he promised, and looked out of the window. 'The American gangsters of the air have no mercy even on women and children. Under these conditions we have to look after our personnel.'

"That was a typical sample of national-socialist logic. The Americans were bombing women and children, so there had to be special protection for Gestapo men. Altogether this dangerous game lasted for about three hours. The essence of it was that I had to display a readiness to join them but at the last moment I must appear to be held back by a purely self-centred attitude of caution or some other consideration far removed from ordinary standards of human decency. At one point he nearly cornered me by pointing out with a fair degree of logic that I was actually working for national-socialism as it was, and my attempt to avoid any direct commitment was merely a refusal to face the facts. However, I managed to evade the issue. This tragic problem had been discussed often enough in our own circle, which was naturally a very narrow and trusted one. History had granted our generation no right of choice and to demand any more of us than ordinary decency would have been unrealistic."

My companion broke off and lapsed into deep thought. I poured out more champagne and we again emptied our glasses.

"Do you rule out the idea of heroism?" I asked involuntarily.

"No," he replied quickly. "Heroism is something I would compare with genius, moral genius."

"And what is the conclusion from that?" I asked.

"I believe that heroism always implies a supreme act of reason, practical action, but a scientist who refused to work for Hitler would not make his protest heard further than the nearest Gestapo office."

"But one doesn't have to give a direct refusal," I said.

182

"An indirect refusal would be pointless. Nobody would understand such a gesture and there would always be someone else to fill the gap when the person in question was eventually removed, if there was a gap to fill."

"All right," I said. "But even if no one notices his removal, he can still refuse for the sake of his own conscience, can he not?"

"I don't know," he said, and gave me a rather strange look. "I have never heard of such a case. That's far too abstract, too maximalist. Something out of *The Karamazov Brothers*... But I know that in your country you take a different view of heroism too."

"We believe that heroism can be inculcated," I replied with some relief at getting back to a less complex subject. I had begun to think that he was misunderstanding me.

"I don't think so," he shook his head. "Under our conditions, the conditions of fascism, it would have been quite wrong and even harmful to ask a person, particularly a scientist, to offer heroic resistance to the regime. If you put the issue that way — either heroic resistance to fascism or complete involvement in it — what you are doing, as a friend of mine once remarked, is to completely disarm people morally. There were some scientists who at first condemned our conciliatory tactics, then gave up the whole thing and concentrated on making a career. Say what you like, but common decency is a great thing."

"But common decency could not defeat the regime?"

"Of course, not."

"Then where's the solution?"

"In this case the solution was provided by the Red Army," he said, and his asymmetrical face broke into a smile.

"But if Hitler had been more careful and not attacked us?"

"He could have chosen a different time, but that's not the point. The point is that the very victories he achieved in such feverish haste were the result of the corruption of a regime which even without the Red Army could not have lasted more than two or three generations. But that was just the situation in which what I call decency would have acquired even greater significance as a means of preserving

183

the nation's moral fibre for a more or less opportune historical moment."

"We are getting away from the subject," I said. "What happened to you after that?"

"Well, to put it briefly," he resumed, lighting another cigarette, "the hunt for my soul lasted about three hours, in the course of which he left the room and returned several times. In the end we both got tired and he suddenly marched me off to someone I took to be his boss. We entered a huge waiting room with a middle-aged woman, a rather plump brunette, sitting at a desk loaded with telephones. Three other people were waiting in the room and I recognised one of them as the man who had come in for the file. The woman was speaking on the telephone. She was talking to her daughter. Apparently the girl had just come home from a picnic and was pouring out an excited story. I could feel that even at some distance from the phone. It was rather strange to hear such things in a place like this. Then a bell rang on the desk.

"'All right, that's enough for now,' I heard the woman say as she put down the receiver. She stood up and walked quickly into the office. The four Gestapo men drew themselves up respectfully. Two minutes later she reappeared.

"'Go inside,' she said and, as she went back to her desk, gave me a look that set my nerves on edge. Only a woman can give you that kind of look. Such a vicious look, I mean. No, there was none of the hatred or contempt that I could expect at any moment from those other four. That look of hers consisted of a feline curiosity in my guts on the one hand, and complete confidence in her master, on the other. It may have been the effect of fatigue, but I actually felt as if my guts might at any moment rise into my throat.

"We went into the office It was an even more luxurious chamber with an even bigger desk loaded with telephones of various colours, and an inkstand shaped like the ruins of an old castle. A big man, who looked rather like the manager of a flourishing restaurant, was sitting at the desk. He was darkhaired and wore a fawn suit with a flamboyant necktie.

"He offered no one a seat and we remained standing by the door. The three men from the waiting room, closer to the desk, and I with my escort a little further away.

"'So he can't make up his mind?' the chief boomed thunderously, staring at me with astonished eyes. 'A promising young scientist and he won't co-operate with us? I just can't believe it!' he exclaimed, and suddenly rose to his full, impressive height.

"His astonished eyes seemed to implore me to deny this false and perhaps even maliciously invented information that his assistants had supplied. As soon as he spoke, I realised he was aping Goering. This was a fashion among functionaries of the Reich in those days. Each of them chose for himself the mask of one of the leaders.

"'And this at a time when hordes of Asiatics are hurling themselves at the sacred soil of Germany, at a time when gangsters of the air are bombing innocent children to death!' He motioned towards the window and to the field beyond where the children were still playing football. They must have been different children by this time, but it seemed to me that both the field and the children had been cultivated specially by the Gestapo for purposes of illustration.

"'I am not refusing,' I began, but he interrupted me.

"'Do you hear that? Didn't I tell you?' he exclaimed. He seemed about to jump on the desk in his enthusiasm. But his tone changed soon enough when he addressed his assistants. 'So you failed to explain to him where his duty lies. You couldn't find the key that exists for every German heart.'

"He looked at me with his bovine eyes and I could see that he was asking for my consent not so much for me to work for them but as a boost to his pedagogical prestige. Let us both put these incompetent devils to shame, he seemed to be suggesting — the murderous clown.

"'You see, it's like this...' I began, sensing that this pedagogical process was going to cost me dear. But just at that moment, to my good fortune, the door opened. He glared at the door like an infuriated bull. It was the secretary.

"'Berlin,' she said softly, and nodded towards one of the telephones.

"He seized the receiver, and it was immediately obvious that we had all vanished from the face of the earth and even he, as he bent over the phone, had correspondingly diminished in stature.

"We withdrew silently to the waiting room, and from the

waiting room into the corridor. The secretary ignored us completely.

"I returned with the fisher of my soul to his office. I felt that he was utterly fed up with me. I also sensed that both he and his colleagues were at heart glad that their chief had failed in his pedagogical efforts. My man made no further attempt to argue with me.

"He signed my permission to leave, wrote a telephone down on a slip of paper, and said, 'If you make up your mind, ring this number.'

"'All right,' I said, and left the room. I don't remember how I found my way home. As I walked through the streets I felt the kind of weakness and pleasure that one experiences on first getting up after a long illness. When I was sure that no one was following me, I tore up the slip of paper and threw it into a refuse bin, though for some reason I still tried to remember the number.

"The next day I did not telephone, of course. But every day after that I lived in a state of constant suspense. One evening when I came home from work my wife said that the phone had rung but, when she had answered it, someone had put the receiver down at the other end. A few days later I myself answered the phone and again there was no reply, or rather I heard someone carefully replace the receiver. Or perhaps it was my imagination.

"I didn't know what to think. In the street and in buses I began to have the impression that there was a detective's eye upon me.

"At the entrance to the institute I would feel nervous if the guard on duty took more than usual interest in my pass.

"Two or three months went by. One day an old school friend of mine rang up. He was now a well-known criminal lawyer and lived in Berlin. As usual we agreed to meet for a walk in town and then go back to my house for dinner. My wife was delighted. His company always had a good effect on me and now I particularly needed something to liven me up.

"He was a witty talker, rather frivolous, but always a good friend. Whenever he visited us from Berlin he would bring with him a whole collection of anecdotes that gave us a better idea of what was going on in the Reich than any other type of information.

"On this occasion he rang off with his usual 'Heil Hitler, thank you for your attention', referring to the fact that all hotel telephones were monitored. For the first time in all these weeks I found myself smiling broadly. I, too, was convinced that my telephone was being tapped.

"My friend and I had similar views on everything that was happening in Germany. Incidentally, he was the only person I had told about my student escapade.

"'I don't believe the Reich is going to last a thousand years but it'll last quite long enough for our generation,' he would say when we talked about it. Like everyone with a gift for humour he was a pessimist. During the past year the information from the Eastern Front had made it look as if he had overrated the Reich's potential. When I had told him this during his previous visit, he had disagreed.

"'On the contrary,' he had exclaimed. 'I underrated the extent of Hitler's madness.'

"We met in the lounge of his hotel. As soon as we were out in the street and at a safe distance, I said, 'Well, start away. Hitler goes into an air-raid shelter and there...'

"'My God!' he exclaimed. 'Only night watchmen tell that kind of story nowadays. The latest thing is the Carpet-eater series.'

"'What's that?' I asked.

"'Listen,' he said, and started on one story after another. Their general theme was that Hitler, on hearing the news of fresh defeats on the Eastern Front, would throw himself on the floor of his study and bite the carpet. We passed several blocks and he was still relating stories from what seemed a quite inexhaustible series. The last one he told, which was far from the best, has engraved itself on my memory.

"Hitler goes into a shop to buy a new carpet. 'Shall I wrap it up for you, or do you wish to gnaw it on the premises?' asks the salesman.

"He had just told this story, when my Gestapo man appeared round the corner coming towards me. In my confusion I could not make up my mind whether to greet him or not. At the last moment I realised that this would be the wrong thing to do, but then I noticed that my friend and he had nodded to each other.

"We walked on. My mind was in a whirl. He went on

talking but I could not understand a word. His voice seemed to come from far away. Feverish thoughts raced through my head. He was working for the Gestapo. They had called him as a witness. I should be shot.

"And yet I still clung to the hope that the Gestapo man was merely a chance acquaintance of his. Perhaps they had met in connection with one of his cases. He had often told me that the Gestapo interfered in political and criminal trials alike.

"But how could I find out? The realisation came to me in a flash. It was quite simple. I must ask him straight out. If they had met by chance he would say who he was, but if they had a secret connection he would, of course, invent something.

"'By the way, who was that you nodded to?' I asked a few minutes later. Oh God, how much depended on his answer. How I would have hugged him if only he had told me the whole truth!

"'Oh, just someone I happen to know,' he replied with studied indifference. I felt his momentary hesitation and all the rest seemed to take place in a mist. There was an air-raid warning. We ran for cover. Near a gutted building we spotted an old air-raid shelter that had caved in on one side.

"He pushed me inside and slithered down the concrete steps after me. Anti-aircraft guns barked overhead. A bomb burst some distance away and I felt the earth give a frightening heave. Gradually the anti-aircraft fire moved away to another part of the town and the sound of bursting bombs grew fainter.

"It's bad enough to die in an air-raid, I thought, but how much worse to be murdered by the Gestapo. Not so much because of the torture. There was something mystical about it. Like being strangled by a ghost.

"Perhaps this was because you were isolated from everyone else and punished in the name of the whole country.

"But what had I done? I had merely written what every educated person in the country knew already. Had I invented new rules for the German language? And why is it that something which everyone of us sees separately cannot be seen by all of us together? But what really worried me was this sense of guilt. Why should I feel that? There must have been some point when I had tacitly, unknowingly agreed to play this game? Otherwise why should I feel guilty?

"We were still sitting on the cold concrete floor, which was strewn with brick rubble. In the semidarkness the broken brick looked like stains of blood on the floor.

"'Oh, hell!' he said, and began to brush himself down. 'This seems to be something one never really gets used to.' He rummaged in his overcoat and took out a packet of cigarettes.

"'Have a smoke?'

"'No,' I said. He flicked his lighter several times before he got a flame, then his round head stood out plainly against the glow of the cigarette. Just like target, I thought suddenly, as it melted into the darkness. The decision formed spontaneously in my mind. His head will show up like that another three times, I decided, and I'll do it. And yet after the third time I felt I must ask him once again.

"'Listen, Emil,' I said. 'Who was that you nodded to in the street?'

"He must have noticed something in my voice. I sensed it in the damp, menacing stillness of the shelter. Soil trickled down between the beams of the roof. I heard the tiny grains pattering on the floor.

"'Well, he was a Gestapo man, if you must know. What of it?' he said. Everything seemed to go limp inside me.

"'How did you come to know him?' I asked.

"'We were at college together. He was offered the job in his last year and he thought fit to ask my advice about it.'

"'Did you give him any?'

"'Are you mad?' he shouted suddenly. 'If a man asks your advice on whether to join the Gestapo, it means he has already decided to join. It would be crazy to advise him against it. Still, what is all this about?'

"'Give me a cigarette,' I said. He held out the packet in the darkness. Only then did I notice that my right hand had been clutching a heavy lump of brick. I released my grip on its cold, slimy surface. Emil appeared not to notice. I told him everything.

"'And you could think that of me?' he said offendedly.

"'Why didn't you tell me the truth straightaway?' I countered.

189

"I felt him staring at me intently in the darkness.

"'It was rather unpleasant to have to tell you I knew someone in the Gestapo,' he said, after a pause. I felt a slight chill had come between us. He must have felt the same.

"Soil was still sprinkling off the ceiling.

"'It seems to have quietened down,' he said, standing up. 'Let's get out of here before the whole place collapses on top of us.'

"And all at once I was overcome by laughter. Either it was hysterics or simply a kind of relief. I had remembered the safe shelter the Gestapo man had offered me. Somehow I had recalled everything they had promised Germany and what they were still promising her, and the whole history of Germany over the past decade struck me as monstrously absurd.

"'I don't know what you find to laugh at,' Emil said, when we were above ground again. 'Look what they have done to us.'

"'I can see,' I said, not realising at the time the full significance of his words. And the significance of them was, apart from anything else, that our friendship was over. He had been ashamed to tell me that he was acquainted with a Gestapo man, and because of that I had not been ashamed to think that he might betray me. Perhaps that was too little to end a friendship? Actually it was more than enough. Friendship does not like being tested. Testing degrades it and destroys its value. If friendship demands testing, some kind of substantial guarantee, it means that it is nothing more than an exchange of certain intellectual commodities.

"Friendship is not merely trust that can be bought by testing, but a trustfulness that exists before any testing takes place, and at the same time it is a happiness, a delight in the very fulness of giving spiritually to a person who is near to one.

"If I say I am a friend of this man it means that I trust him utterly and completely because my feeling implies a realisation of the great fraternal predestination of man. And as for tests — should fate send them, they will be only a confirmation of that surmise, and not a signed and sealed recommendation of a partner's good faith. But I think I have been talking too much...."

"Let's drink to that never happening again," I said, taking advantage of his unexpected pause. I felt that his reminiscences had overexcited him and we were beginning to attract attention.

"Yes, let's drink to that," he agreed, apparently somewhat embarrassed at having told such a long story.

We drank. The champagne was tepid by now and my toast did not strike me as very convincing.

My acquaintance had obviously tired himself with his recollections and seemed a little bemused. To revive him I said that the previous autumn I had visited West Germany, where the thing that had struck me most had been the friendliness of ordinary Germans towards our delegation. He nodded, and seemed to be pleased at this information. And then he was brilliant once more, if what he had been relating up to then could be called brilliant.

"We, Germans," he said, barely restraining a smile that now seemed not half so asymmetrical, if asymmetrical at all, "are very slow to lose our respect for the big stick."

This set us both laughing. And perhaps we should have gone on laughing for eternity had I not noticed that people were coming up towards us from the pier. Apparently the launch had arrived.

"Ooo-hoo!" he exclaimed with a kind of plaintive dignity and hurried off to the pier.

From this strange sound that had risen so suddenly from the depths of his German soul I concluded that he had had quite enough of the Russian language and decided to call it a day.

Some of the holiday-makers were still walking along the pier when he reached it. I heard them greeting each other loudly from a distance and scraps of their noisy conversation. We, Russians, had also greeted one another in this noisy fashion while travelling in Germany. Once you get accustomed to the idea that no one around you understands the language you are speaking, you even forget that they can hear it.

The pensioner was still sitting at the table with his faded lady friend. I felt his gaze upon me.

"So he's a German?" he asked in surprise.

"Yes," I said. "What of it?"

"Well, I thought he was Estonian," he observed with a touch of annoyance, as though, if he had only been informed beforehand, he might have been able to do something about it.

"Democratic or Federal?" he asked a moment later in a tone that dismissed the possibility of taking any action but showed a desire to know the extent of the error he had committed.

"Federal," I said.

"What does he say about Kiesinger?" he asked unexpectedly, leaning towards me with a kind of communal curiosity.

"Nothing," I said.

"Aha! Humph," the pensioner pronounced with sly pomposity and shook his pink head.

I laughed. The old man was really rather amusing. He also broke into silent triumphant laughter.

"What could he tell us anyway?" he said, addressing his companion between chuckles. "We know all about it from the newspapers as it is."

The German came smilingly to the table with his wife and daughter. He introduced us and purely for the sake of rhetoric I proposed another bottle. His wife shook her head and, lifting a brown young arm, pointed to her watch. Like all of them, she was wearing a very low-cut dress and looked youthful and athletic. It was rather strange to see a woman who had lived through a whole epoch in the history of her people and looked none the worse for it. As for the girl, I had the impression that she would have been only too glad of some champagne if her parents had agreed. Her father and I shook hands firmly and they went off in the direction of a hotel.

"We won the war and they go about enjoying themselves," said the pensioner, and laughed goodnaturedly as he watched them go.

I made no reply.

"If you like," he said, addressing his companion much more sternly, "I can bring you a book tomorrow by the French Academician André Maurois *The Life and Adventures of Georges Sand.*

"Yes, I should like that," she replied.

"That's a rare book too," the pensioner said. "It describes all her lovers, to wit — Frederick Chopin, Prosper Merimé, Alfred de Musset...."

He paused, trying to remember the rest of Georges Sand's lovers.

"Maupassant," the woman suggested doubtfully.

"In the first place, you should say not Maupassant but Guy de Maupassant," he corrected her sternly. "And secondly, he is not included, although a number of other great European figures are there."

"I shall be extremely grateful," the woman responded, gently evading any further discussion.

"You should indeed, it's a rare book," the pensioner observed and dropped his beads into his tunic pocket. "Wait for me here at the same time tomorrow."

"I'll make a point of it," the woman said respectfully.

"Expect me," the pensioner repeated and, inclining his pink pate, stalked away across the boulevard.

The woman watched him go, and then asked me rather anxiously, "Do you think he'll come?"

"Of course, he will," I said. "What else can he do with himself?"

"There are all sorts, you know," the woman sighed. She sat stolidly at her table and now seemed very big and lonely.

I paid the bill and went off to a coffee-house. The sun had sunk rather low over the sea. The launch that had brought the wife and daughter of the German physicist left almost empty for the beach. When I reached the coffee-house I found the pensioner there, already surrounded by a gang of other old men. Among their withered coffee-coloured faces his pink countenance displayed a rubicund independence.

CATCHING TROUT ON THE UPPER KODOR

I awoke early and remembered that the evening before I had made up my mind to go fishing for trout. Probably it was this that had woken me. I raised my head and looked round. The lads were all sleeping in the strangest attitudes as though sleep had caught them by surprise, certain movements half-completed. A lilac dawn showed through the window. It was still very early. The bare log walls glowed faintly golden and smelled of fresh resin.

All the week we had been trekking in the mountains, visiting places where there had been fighting in defence of the Caucasus. The expedition had been planned long ago by students of our Geography Faculty and was led by my friend Avtandil Tsikridze, a physical training instructor. It was he who had suggested I should join them. I had gladly agreed.

On our last day, spurred on by lack of food — somebody had miscalculated student appetites — we had done our longest hike and by evening reached this village.

Fortunately, we did not have to pitch our tents because the local militia chief had hospitably provided us with accommodation for the night in what was either a former store-shed or a future club-house. He appeared, fishing rod in hand, when we, having dumped our rucksacks, were lolling blissfully on the grass over a bend in the river.

After climbing down the steep slope, he set about making his casts in a businesslike fashion, evidently into pools with which he was thoroughly familiar. He would make a cast, wiggle his rod a bit, and pull out a trout. Then he would walk on a few paces, make another cast, jerk and wiggle his rod again — and out came another trout. From a distance it looked as if he was simply pricking out the fish with the long thin needle of his fishing line. Having caught a dozen fine trout in the space of half an hour, he quite suddenly, for no apparent reason, as though he had collected his day's quota, reeled in his line and came up to us.

That evening, despite our weariness one of the students and I cut ourselves rods from a hazel bush and fitted them out with lines. The student's name was Lusik. In some Abkhazian villages they give their children Russian names or simply call them by some Russian word, usually a resounding one often repeated on the radio. For instance, I used to know a lad whose name was Voina (war). Possibly a little worried by his own name, he always behaved in a markedly peaceful manner.

Lusik was the same. As though bewitched by his feminine name, he was shy and stood out among the other lads by a scrupulous respectfulness that never degenerated into servility. He was sturdy as a little donkey, and his amazing stamina had put to shame the toughest members of our expedition, which included two trained athletes.

...I took a big clasp-knife out of my rucksack and two matchboxes, one with some fish eggs in it, and the other with spare hooks, and pushed the rucksack back against the wall.

The matchbox of spawn had been given to me by a man who had come up to our fire when we were camped at the foot of Marukh.

He had arrived in a helicopter belonging to a party of geologists who had set up camp here before us and were working in this locality. He was a fair-haired man of about thirty, already running to fat. He was wearing new shorts and heavy, also new, climbing boots, and carried an ice-axe. For some two hours he sat with us by the fire, taking an unobtrusive interest in us and our expedition. He did mention his name, but I immediately forgot it. One of the lads, choosing the right moment, asked him where he worked.

"In a certain high-level department," he said smiling amiably, as if hinting at the relative nature of departmental heights compared with the height we were now at. The pun received no further explanation, but then we were not particularly interested in where he worked anyway.

The next morning, when we were packing up to go,

he brought me this matchbox full of spawn. The evening before he had heard me complaining that the local trout were not attracted by grasshoppers and for some reason worms were hard to come by.

"I suppose the earth, like any other product, gets worm-eaten in the warmer places," I had remarked to my own surprise.

He nodded understandingly, although I myself was not too clear about the implications of my schizophrenic image. And the next morning he brought me the spawn.

I was touched by his thoughtfulness and regretted that I had forgotten his name, but it would have been awkward to ask again at this juncture. Anyway I made an effort to show that I believed in his work in a certain high-level department, although he may not have noticed it. That is, he may not have noticed my effort.

When we went off in single file with our rucksacks on our backs, he stood by the helicopter in his new shorts with his ice-axe in one hand and a Svan hat, also new, in the other and waved good-bye with the hat and I finally forgave him for his innocent Alpine masquerade. Especially as all this put together, he and the helicopter on the green meadow surrounded by the stern mountains, looked superb and could have been used as an advertisement for air tourism.

...I buttoned up the pockets of my rucksack, ran my hands over my clothing, trying to remember anything I might have forgotten, and stood up. I decided not to wake Lusik. He'll come if he wakes up, I thought. Perhaps he has changed his mind, and anyhow it's better to fish on one's own.

On the table lay several loaves of white bread with glowing russet crusts. The militia chief had gone to the village shopkeeper in the evening and he had opened his shop to provide us with bread, butter, sugar and macaroni. Bread in such quantity was a pleasant sight.

I went up to the table, took out my knife and cut off a big crust. The bread resisted resiliently and with a little squeak as I cut it. One of the lads without waking, smacked his lips and it seemed to me, as if this was his response to the sound of bread being cut. There was also a small cask of butter. I spread butter thickly over the crust, took a bite out of it and involuntarily glanced at the lad who had smacked his lips. This time he had felt nothing.

I went out on to the veranda and knocked the knife on the rail to close it. For some reason it would not close any other way.

Only then did I notice that Lusik was standing by the porch steps, where the fishing rods were leaning against the wall.

"Been up long?" I asked, chewing.

"No," he answered hastily, looking up at me with his big phoenix-like eyes. I could see he was afraid that I might feel embarrassed to find him here waiting for me.

"Go and cut yourself a slice," I said, and offered him the knife.

"I don't want any," Lusik said, shaking his head.

"Go on," I repeated, biting into my crust again.

"I swear by my mother that I don't like eating so early," Lusik said, wrinkling his nose and raising his eyebrows almost to his schoolboy fringe.

"Let's go and dig for worms then," I said, and walked down the steps.

Lusik picked up both rods and followed me.

We walked along the village street. On our left were the public buildings, the collective farm management office, the restaurant, and the barn with its amber, freshly planed log walls. They all stood on the edge of a cliff. From below came the roar of the invisible river. On the right was a maize field. The maize was ripening and the shucks were sticking out from the well-formed cobs. The street was deserted except for three pigs of the local breed, black and long like artillery shells, that were slowly crossing it.

The sky was a pale-green, exquisitely tender. Ahead of us to the south shone a huge bedraggled star. There were no other stars and this solitary one looked as if it had somehow got left behind. As I walked down the road I kept admiring this big wet star that seemed to be ashamed of its bigness.

The mountains, as yet untouched by the sun, were a sombre blue. Only a small golden spot on the jagged peak of the highest was ablaze.

197

Beyond the maize field on the right there was a school yard in which there stood a small, very homely village school. The door of one of the classrooms was open. All the classrooms opened on to a long veranda with a porch. At one end of the veranda there was a pile of desks standing one atop the other.

A track ran past the school yard in the direction of the street. It was scattered with pebbles and large stones carried down by heavy rains.

Here we decided to make our first search. While I was still finishing my buttered crust, Lusik propped the rods against the fence and started heaving the stones.

"Anything there?" I asked when he had lifted the first stone and was peering under it. He was still holding it half raised as though, if there turned out to be no worms under it, he was going to put it back in exactly the same position.

"Yes, there are," Lusik said, and heaved the stone away.

I swallowed my last mouthful and felt in need of a smoke but, remembering that I had only three cigarettes in the breast pocket of my shirt, I decided to try and last out. I took out the matchbox that was in the same pocket, tipped the matches out of it and kept the empty box ready for the worms. Lusik was already collecting his in a tin.

Turning up the boulders in this fashion we gradually made our way up the track. There were not many worms to be had and under some of the stones there were none at all. Little Lusik sometimes shifted really massive boulders. You could see his arms were used to hard work. In fact, everything about his sturdy stubborn little figure suggested that he was used to overcoming the resistance of gravity.

As we moved gradually up the track we drew level with the school. When I raised my head for a moment I noticed a woman on the veranda. She was squeezing a wet rag out into a pail. I was surprised that I had not noticed her before, and even more surprised to see that she was a fair-haired Russian woman. That was unusual here.

"Good morning," I said, when she turned her head.

"Good morning," she replied amiably, but without any sign of curiosity.

A girl in her teens came out of the open classroom

carrying a besom. She dipped it in the pail, shook it and having whacked the steps with it a few times, gave us a silent look and went back into the classroom. She was beautiful and walked away with her back perfectly straight conscious of being looked at. The charm of her face lay, probably, in the rare combination it achieved of oriental brilliance and a Slav softness of feature.

I looked at Lusik. He was staring open-mouthed with his innocent phoenix-like eyes.

"Where did she spring from?" he asked me in Abkhazian.

"Come back in about three years' time," I said.

Lusik sighed and set about lifting the next stone. I bent down with him.

I could hear the woman scrubbing the veranda floor with her rag and sluicing it with water. It must have been the postwar shortages that drove her up here into this remote mountain village, I thought. Then she had this girl by some Svan and stayed on here, I decided, surprising myself by my own insight.

"How do we get down to the river from here?" I asked.

She straightened up and eased her head back to relax her neck muscles.

"Over there." She held out a bare arm that was wet to the elbow. "You'll find the way down as soon as you get to that house."

"I know it," Lusik said.

The girl with the besom appeared again.

"Is that your daughter?" I asked.

"My eldest," the woman affirmed with a quiet pride.

"Why, have you any others?"

"Six altogether," she smiled.

That was a real surprise. She looked far too young for a woman who had borne six children.

"Oh! Does your husband work at the school?"

"He's the chairman of the collective farm," she corrected me and added, with another nod towards the house across the road, "That's our house."

It was barely visible through the fruit-trees but I could see that it was the kind of roomy well-built place that might belong to the farm chairman.

"My regular job's at the weather station," she explained. "This is just something I do on the side."

The girl, who had been listening to the conversation, knocked out her besom against the porch steps and with a severe glance at her mother returned to the classroom, still keeping her back very stiff and straight.

"Pretty hard for you, isn't it?" I asked, trying to include in my question household matters, the children and, above all, living among a strange people.

"Not so bad," she said, "my daughter helps..."

We did not talk about anything else. Having collected enough worms, Lusik and I picked up our rods and set off. I glanced round to say good-bye, but now they were carrying the desks into the classroom and had no time for us.

As I walked past the house opposite the school I saw four youngsters with fair hair and dark eyes. They were clinging to the new fence and staring out into the street.

"What is your father?" I asked the eldest, a boy of about six.

"Chairman," he gurgled, and I noticed his fingers tighten round the stakes of the fence.

We turned off the track and made our way down a very steep path. Tiny pebbles went bouncing away from under our feet and sometimes I had to use my rod as a brake. Thickets of hazel, elder and blackberry overhung the path on both sides. One spur of blackberry was so heavily loaded with dark dusty fruit that I could not resist.

I planted my rod on the path and, holding it with my chin to stop it slipping away, carefully bent the branch and gathered a handful of berries. Having puffed the dust off them, I poured the cool sweet berries into my mouth. There were plenty more on the branch but I decided not to let myself be diverted and took to the path. The sound of the river was becoming more audible and I was eager to reach the bank.

Lusik was waiting for me below. As soon as I came out on the bank I felt a rush of cool air on my face. It was the air stream carried by the whirling waters.

The nearness of the water spurred us on and we crunched over the pebbles of the dried-up channels towards it. About ten metres from the water I signed to Lusik not to talk, and trying not to make so much noise on the pebbles, we crept to the water's edge. An experienced angler had taught me this. I had been amused at the sight of him crawling down to the water as if he were stalking game, but when he fished out a score of trout and I caught no more than a couple of miserable troutlets in a whole day I had to believe in the advantage of experience.

Lusik was making signs and pointing. I looked downstream and saw a lad with a fishing rod about fifty metres away. I recognised him at once as one of our party.

It was unpleasant that he had forestalled us. We had not even known that he intended to go fishing. As if sensing our gaze, he looked round. I made an inquiring gesture: how goes it? He replied with a limp wave of the arm: nothing doing. I thought I glimpsed a frown of disappointment on his face. He turned away and applied himself to his rod.

If that's how it is, I thought, we can consider that he arrived with us and we began fishing at the same time. After all, the fish don't know he was here first... I signed to Lusik to go on downstream and keep his distance from me. He did so.

I took the matchbox out of my waterproof jacket, selected a fat worm and fixed it on the hook, leaving its tail wiggling.

At this spot the river split in two, forming a long island overgrown with grass and stunted alders. The main channel was on the other side. The near channel began with a shallow rapid, below which I noticed a small deep pool. I crept over to it and, holding the line by the sinker with one hand, drew the rod back with the other to judge the length of my cast more exactly. Then I swung the rod gently and let go of the line. The sinker plummeted neatly into the pool.

Now the main thing is not to get snagged, I thought, trying to take in the slack so that the hook was not carried round an underwater rock or branch. Something plucked at the line and my hand gave an involuntary jerk. The hook came up with nothing on it. After a few more false alarms I realised that this was due not to a fish biting, but to the tugging of underwater currents; but my wrist still jerked

201

each time as if from an electric shock. My mind was always a fraction of a second behind the reflex.

Tap! I felt the faint tug and forced my hand to keep still.

Still crouching on my heels and very excited, I waited for another bite, impressing on myself that I should not jerk my hand when I felt it.

He'll try again in a minute, I told myself, but be patient. The fish did nibble the bait again and my hand scarcely moved. This time the fish was more careful. That's good, I thought, keep that up a few times until you feel that it's taken the bait.

The fish attacked again, I made my strike and the next moment a wet, gleaming trout was fluttering in the air. I swung the rod towards the bank and the line with the heavy fish dancing on the end of it came before my eyes. In my excitement I did not seize it at once. Eventually I reached out and got a firm grip on that cold living body, laid my rod down carefully, and holding the fish even more tightly, with my other hand freed the hook from its soundlessly hiccupping mouth.

I had never caught such a big one before. It was the size of a full-grown corn cob. Its back was speckled with red spots. I carefully unbuttoned the flap of my jacket pocket, dropped it in and buttoned the pocket again. In the pocket it writhed with fresh strength. I had a knife there and decided that it might bruise itself on the haft. So I opened the pocket again and with the coldness of the fish on the back of my hand took the knife out, transferred it to another pocket and again buttoned the flap over the fish.

I straightened up, feeling a need for distraction after such a large and almost sickening dose of happiness. I took a deep breath and looked round. The water was noticeably lighter and the airstream above it had warmed a little. The mountains on the other side of the river lay in sombre blue shadow but the peaks of those behind me were a blaze of gold.

Lusik was not far away downstream. I realised that he had not seen anything, otherwise he would still be looking in my direction. Lusik had never done any fishing before, except for a couple of attempts at trout up here with me in the mountains. But there had been no catch, so he had not yet experienced the real thrill.

You seldom find an angler among the Abkhazians. This is a strange thing for a people who have lived by the sea for centuries. I think it was not always so. The unfortunate migration to Turkey in the last century probably took with it most of the inhabitants of the coast and the river valleys and with their departure the Abkhazian fishing industry came to a sudden end.

If such blank spots, such oblivion can occur in a people's memory of such a visible thing as fishing, I thought, how carefully must we guard the more fragile values against the danger of disappearance, evaporation...

The student who had arrived before us had changed his ground.

He had told me once that he and his father had a motor boat and often went fishing at sea. I had asked him if he ever sold fish because with a motor boat you can nearly always find a shoal and there are plenty of fish to be caught when trolling in a good shoal.

He looked straight into my eyes and said that he and his father *never* sold fish. I felt that he was offended. But there had been no offence meant.

I baited my hook again and made a cast. Now I fished standing up. I felt that the expedition was going to be a good one. I don't know why, but I was sure of it.

In a little while I again felt a nibbling, and tried to keep my hand still. There were a few more stirrings, then stillness, but I went on waiting, determined to outwit the fish. When I pulled in the line, however, the bait was gone. The fish must have quietly nibbled it away and I had been waiting for it to snap at a bare hook.

I baited the hook again and made a careful cast. The line circled smoothly in the eddying waters of the pool and I kept it there with a light flick of the rod whenever it floated away. When there was still no bite, I decided to let the bait go downstream a little, then drew it back against the current to tempt some of the bolder fish.

The trout that I had caught was slapping me on the belly and every slap helped me to be patient.

At last I caught a medium-sized trout and put it in my pocket. The first one, which had been still for a while, began to flap about with the second. It must be glad of the company,

I thought, perhaps it has given it fresh hope. But then I decided that the second trout had brought the first to life with its wet oxygenated gills. I squatted down, opened my pocket and poured in a few handfuls of water.

Now the two trout flapped about in the water and from time to time nudged me almost gratefully in the stomach, giving me a strange sensation of rather foolish joy.

There seemed to be nothing more going for me on this spot, so I decided to move on. I drew in my line, wound it round the rod and planted the hook in the soft fresh wood.

I might have tried upstream, but the cliffs on either side fell straight into the water and there was no way round them. Further up the river the bank was much more accessible, but it could not be reached from here. I moved downstream.

By now the sun was shining brightly and gave a pleasant warmth. A mist was creeping up from behind one of the mountains. In the shallows the water was clear and every pebble shone joyfully, casting a quivering shadow on the sandy bottom. Now and then for no apparent reason little underwater tornados whipped up the sand.

I came up to Lusik. Waist deep in the water, he was leaning over and groping in it with an alert expression in his big, phoenix-like eyes. His clothes were lying neatly folded on the bank.

"Snagged up?" I asked as I approached.

"I can't reach it," he said in an unexpectedly old-mannish voice. The poor fellow was hoarse from the cold. "Come out," I said and picked up his rod.

"I'll lose the hook," Lusik croaked, just like a thrifty old man, and climbed reluctantly out of the water.

He was almost black with cold.

I pulled the line till it broke, selected a new hook and tied it on. Holding the hook in one hand, I put the other end of the tie between my teeth, tugged it tight and actually bit off the end, which I was not usually able to do.

"There we are," I said, spitting out the end.

"Have you caught anything?" Lusik asked with his teeth chattering.

"Two," I said, and opened my jacket pocket. Lusik put his hand in and pulled out the big one. It was still alive.

"What a whopper," he croaked, shivering. "I can feel them nibbling, but they don't bite."

"Don't hurry over your strike," I said, and when he had replaced the trout in my pocket went down to the edge and poured in a few more handfuls of fresh water.

"Aren't we going yet?" Lusik asked.

"No fear," I said, and walked on down the bank.

"I'll stay a bit longer, then go back. The lads will be waiting," Lusik shouted after me. His voice was coming through clearer now.

I nodded without looking round and walked on. Far ahead I caught a glimpse of the other student. He had again shifted his position. He kept on shifting it — a sure sign of failure.

I wanted to be left quite alone and decided not to try any more until I had passed the student. I was sure he had disturbed all the fish around here and it would be no use trying, although there were some very good pools.

At one of them I did stop to make a cast. I got a bite straight away, but after that came a lull. Grudging the time I was wasting and yet determined to turn it to some use, I went on waiting stubbornly.

Snap! Snap! It was double bite. I made my strike and pulled out a trout. Good for you, I told myself, you had the patience and here's your reward.

But as soon as I tried to get my hand to it the fish wriggled off the hook and fell on the bank. I dropped my rod and tried to grab it, but with a desperate agility it slipped away into the water. In its terror it seemed to have grown feet on its belly.

Cursing myself for the delay, I reeled in my line somehow and set off downstream almost at a run.

The student was fishing knee-deep in the shallows. Here the river was racing noisily over a series of small rapids, and he did not hear me approach. His whole posture suggested that he had no faith in the enterprise and was merely amusing himself for want of something better to do.

"How's it going?" I shouted.

He turned and shook his head.

"How about you?" he asked.

The river drowned the sound of his voice and I indicated

with my fingers that I had caught two fish, then pulled the big trout out of my pocket to show him.

I went on further and decided not to stop until I found the finest spot of all.

This was a huge pinkish-lilac boulder. It was separated from the bank by a narrow strip of water. On one side I could see a deep pool and I guessed that there must be another deep, quiet backwater on the other side.

My excitement returned and I crept over to the boulder, trying not to make a noise on the pebbles. Having silently reached the water's edge I propped the rod against the boulder and sprang on to it.

The boulder was cold and slippery. On this side the dew had not yet dried. I pulled my rod up and climbed cautiously to the top. Here it was dry and on both sides there were deep green pools of quiet water.

Let the bait be worthy of the place, I decided and, trying not to give my presence away, took the matchbox of spawn out of my pocket. I had to press hard to open it. The spawn was of an unusual kind. I had never seen anything like it even on the Kommandorskiye Islands, where people go to collect spawn with pails and baskets, as if they were picking berries. The grains lay in a compact amber-coloured bunch, each as big as a current.

That comrade really must be working in some high-level department, I thought, I wonder what the fish is that spawns such fish eggs. I wish I could ask him.

The sun shone pleasantly warm on my back. The river was murmuring quietly. The green water offered its tempting depths. The grains of spawn gleamed with a noble transparency in the sunlight. I fixed two on the hook, squeezed them a little to make them stick together and still trying not to show myself, made a cast.

For a few seconds the red blob of spawn glimmered in the green mass, then vanished. I felt the sinker hit the bottom, flicked it up a little and waited motionless. After a while I raised the rod a little and drew it back and forth a few times, then let the sinker touch the bottom again. I was trying to give the impression of an alluring Queen Spawn dallying under water.

Snap! I felt the tug on the moving bait and paused in

expectation of a second attack. There was a pause. It was as if the fish couldn't believe how lucky it was to find such a tasty morsel. I gave the rod a flick and the trout touched the bait again. I decided to get my line moving, but on a wider track and without stopping at the first bite, so that the temptation would not merely be moving but going away and thus call for more resolute action.

Snap, snap, snap, snap! I made my strike. The fish tugged back hard in the depths, but I hauled on my rod and a trout was soon flapping in the air. In its own element, when first struggling in the depths and as it came out of the water, it had seemed huge, but it was not actually so big as the first. Still it was pretty big.

As soon as I put it in my pocket, all three fish livened up and flapped about in what was left of the water. It was like a new prisoner bringing life to the exhausted inmates of a gaol.

I looked down at the other side of the boulder. This side was in the sun and the water was lighter, but even so the bottom was not visible. The pool was very deep. I decided to try this side and then fish steadily now on one side, now on the other.

I put two more fish eggs on the hook, sat down in a more comfortable position, so as not to press on my pocketful of fish, and made a cast. The boulder, now pleasantly warmed by the sun, gave off a wholesome flinty smell of healthy old age. I took a cigarette out of my shirt pocket and lighted it.

I enjoyed my cigarette hugely but was a little surprised that nothing rose to the bait. A little further downstream the river divided again, forming a low sandy island with a few tufts of grass and a solitary chestnut-tree twisted in the direction of the current. A good place for sunbathing, I thought. If it got too hot you could always rest in the shade of that tree. Evidently the island was flooded not only in spring but after every heavy rain.

I threw my butt away and waited a little longer, wondering why there was no sign of a bite. Perhaps the line showed up in this sunlit water and the fish were frightened?

I crossed to the other side of the boulder and almost at once caught a huge trout, or so it seemed to me after the long run of bad luck on the other side. It was certainly a big one, bigger than its predecessor, though not, of course, as big as the first. Perhaps that one had been a salmon. And anyway where was the dividing line between a big trout and a small salmon?

I cast my bait and suddenly heard a kind of clicking. "What the devil?" I wondered, and looked round.

About a dozen little children had gathered on the edge of the high cliff above me. Some of them were carrying school cases. When they realised I had noticed them, they burst into a twitter of joy and the ones without cases swung their arms all together. The next moment several fierce little stones clicked and clattered round my boulder.

I shook my fist, which at once put the little band into a frenzy of joy. They jumped and babbled merrily, and those who were still holding their cases dropped them, and a moment later another dozen pebbles came flying down. Not one of them landed on the boulder, but some of them bounced off the pebbles on the bank and in the silliest and most unexpected fashion ricocheted against the boulder and dropped back into the water. I got terribly angry and stood up, this time shaking both fists, which judging from the unanimous howl afforded them utmost delight. Another hail of stones followed.

Then I decided to pretend not to notice them. They shouted several times but I feigned total attention to my rod and line, although what fishing could I do now! I sat with one eye on the bank, where their malicious pebbles were landing regularly to remind me of their presence.

I decided that I had better move. I would cross both streams and come out on the other bank. Most of this bank was visible from the road and I felt that they would not leave me in peace.

As soon as I climbed down from the boulder and walked downstream, a move that was correctly interpreted by those little villains as quitting the field of battle, I heard catcalls and victorious yippeeing behind me.

I found a shallow place, stepped into the stingingly cold water and crossed the first stream. In places the water came up to my waist and pulled me hard. I tried not to stumble, but wet sports boots became very slippery. The fish in my pocket, sensing the nearness of their own element, raised a rumpus.

As I made my way up the bank of the island I heard the far-off ringing of the school bell. I glanced round and saw the diminutive figures of those little bandits running along the road. Well, damn it all, I thought, and suddenly burst out laughing. The water had cooled my fury. But now I had no desire to turn back. I went on, crossed the second stream and came out on the narrow green bank. It was hemmed by a forest of beech and cedar. Higher up the stream a huge beech-tree was leaning almost horizontally over the water. Its green branches hung comfortingly over the swirling currents.

As there seemed to be no good spot close by I decided to try fishing in the main stream. There was nothing to worry about now because I was wet through already. I baited the hook, chose the deepest spot by eye and went as near to it as I could.

Nothing rose. I was about to climb out on to the bank when I felt that the line had caught on something. I decided to sacrifice the hook and pulled. The line tautened, broke and came to the surface. It was the sinker, not the hook that had caught.

I emerged from the water with my feet so numb I could scarely walk. As I had no spare sinker, I searched and found a long-shaped pebble, narrow in the middle, and tied it to the line. Of course, it was not much of a substitute, but it was better than nothing. I decided to try from the overhanging beech-tree and headed upstream. It was pleasant to walk on grass after the slippery stones of the riverbed. The water squelched in my boots and sometimes spurted out through the eyelets. The circulation soon returned to my legs and made them warm, but my body felt chilly and shivers chased each other up my spine.

I climbed on to the thick, moss-patched trunk of the tree and walked out along it to the very middle of the stream. The deep green water, splashing gently on the dangling branches, flowed swiftly beneath me. The branches didn't seem to mind being in the water at all.

The deep green flood streamed past below, murmuring softly. Shadows swayed on its surface. A bird, oblivious of my presence, alighted on the branch quite close to me. It was probably a wagtail. At any rate it kept wagging its long tail as it looked around. Having noticed me, or rather realising that I was a living creature, it shot away through the beech leaves.

I lighted a cigarette. Still nothing rose to my bait. I felt that it was much too nice here to expect good fishing as well. Perhaps I had even lost interest in trout. I felt that I had had enough of fishing. I lifted my rod, pulled off the stone, wound the line round the rod and lodged it between two branches.

It seemed a pity to leave. I pushed my heavy pocket of fish aside and lay face down on the sun-warmed tree-trunk. It was swaying slightly under the pressure of the water pulling at its submerged branches. The nearness of the deep swiftly flowing water increased the sense of peace and immobility. A winy smell rose from the sun-warmed trunk. The sun's rays felt steamily hot through my wet trousers. The moss tickled my cheek, the trunk swayed and I fell into a sweet doze. An ant crawled slowly across my neck.

Through my drowsiness I reflected that it was a long time since I had known such peace. Perhaps this was something I had never known. Even with a woman you loved it would not be so peaceful. Perhaps because there was always the danger that she would start talking and spoil everything. But even if she didn't, there would always be a fringe of awareness that she might, and there was no telling how it might end. So you could never experience such complete bliss as you had here. But here you had it because a tree could not possibly begin to talk; that was for sure.

Through drowsiness I heard a distant whistle from the other bank. It seemed to come from another life. Still dozing, I wondered how it could possibly have carried such a distance. The whistle was repeated several times and each time I wondered drowsily how I had managed to hear it.

Then I heard a chanting voice but could not make out the words. Then came more whistling and the chanting voice again. I realised that they both came from one persistent source, and slowly I became aware that the whistling and chanting were produced by several people together...

"Lorry-is-here!" I felt the words rather than heard them. A stab of alarm passed through me. I realised that the lorry that was to pick us up had arrived and the whole group was waiting for me. I grabbed my rod and ran down from the trunk.

The sun was quite high by now. It was probably about eleven o'clock. I had quite forgotten the time and now felt embarrassed to have kept so many people waiting. Besides, I was afraid they would leave without me. I had no money to pay for the journey back. And when would I pick up a lift anyway?

Without looking for a ford I charged into the water and crossed the first stream almost at a run. After running across the island I plunged into the water again. Here the river was broad and shallow. I ran as fast as I could, trying not to stumble and bruise my legs. I did stumble several times, but always managed to save myself with the rod.

When quite near the bank, I felt the water growing much deeper. I could hardly keep on my feet. "What the devil!" I muttered and halted.

The water was only just above my waist, but the current was so strong that only the rod kept me from being swept away. I regretted that I had not gone back downstream, where I had quite easily forded the river before. At the same time it was hard to believe that I should not be able to manage the last five metres to the bank. I took a step forward, putting all my weight on the rod. The main thing was not to trust your foot until it had found a firm new foothold. Some of the stones rolled over and moved away with the current as soon as I trodded on them. The water rose in a hostile flood around me. And suddenly I realised I could not take a single step because all my strength was needed to hold on where I was.

I felt fear surging up and sweeping away consciousness at terrifying speed. And more afraid of this fear than anything else, I tried to forestall it by action, by leaning into the current and stepping off quickly. The flood snatched me at once and dragged me down. My body sank into the icy murk and I swallowed water.

I managed to regain the surface and feel the bottom, but the current carried me away again while out of sheer obstinacy I went on clutching the rod. I swallowed more water, but this time let go of the rod as soon as I surfaced, and struck

211

out with all my strength. I was still being carried along at terrifying speed and could feel my strength failing. Nevertheless I managed to approach the bank and grab a boulder, though I was sure I hadn't the strength to pull myself out.

But at least I could rest and get my breath back.

At this moment I saw a hand reaching out from above. I clutched it and the two of us together hauled my body out on to the bank.

It was Lusik. I felt dizzy and sick, but sitting on the pebbly beach I slowly recovered.

"I shouted to you," Lusik said, "didn't you hear?"

"No," I said. Perhaps he hadn't seen the whole thing. Perhaps he had just come down to the bank to give me a hand. I didn't want him to know what predicament I had been in.

"We had breakfast long ago, the lorry's waiting," Lusik reminded me patiently.

"All right, just a minute," I said, and stood up with an effort.

I still felt sick from exhaustion. I opened the pocket of my jacket, pulled out the trout and tossed them on the sand. They were still alive. When the current had swept me away they had become gloatingly still. Or perhaps I was imagining it all.

It had been a strange feeling when I was carried away. What a devilish force, I thought, recalling the vicious persistence of the water as it dragged me down.

I was longing for a smoke. I put my hand in my pocket but the cigarette was sodden. I pulled everything out of the pockets, undressed, squeezed out my pants and vest, then dressed again.

Lusik had threaded the trout on to a twig and was waiting patiently. I was quite indifferent to them now.

We set off. Lusik took the lead. The heavy bunch of fresh trout dangled from his hand. The red spots on their backs were still bright. By the time we started climbing I wanted to carry them myself, but I could hardly keep up with Lusik.

"Hand over," I said when he stopped to wait for me at a bend.

"It's all right. I'll carry them," Lusik replied.

But I took the bunch all the same. I felt that it would be more proper for me to appear carrying my own catch, although there would have been no doubt as to where they were.

When we reached the street, everyone was seated in the lorry. Cheerful pandemonium broke out as soon as they saw us and hands reached down from the back to help us in. The student who had been out fishing before us looked disdainfully at the bunch of trout just to show that no one could surprise him with fish.

"I lost one," I announced, holding out the catch to somebody.

The bunch was handed round. Everyone was impressed, but when it came back to me someone said that we had a four hours' journey ahead of us and they would go bad by the time we reached town.

"They'd have made a nice soup for lunch," he added.

"Better fried," someone else suggested.

"Not enough to go round if they were fried," said the other, "but you could make a good fish soup."

I, too, realised that the journey would be too long, specially in the heat. Not that they would really go bad, but it would be a pity to bring this fine bunch of trout to town in a miserable state.

As though sensing my hesitation, a long black pig came up to me. It stood there waiting with feigned patience to see what I was going to do with my catch.

"Give it to the restaurant," someone suggested.

I glanced round. The door of the restaurant was open and loud voices could be heard. I shoved the pig out of my way and walked to the restaurant. It was deserted except for three Svans who were drinking white wine with tomatoes and *suluguni* cheese. They seemed to have drunk quite a lot already. The bartender was engaged in a quarrel with one of them.

I offered him the bunch of trout. Without noticing me, he took my catch, carried it off into the kitchen and came back, still berating one of the drinkers. He just didn't notice me at all. I walked out of the restaurant and climbed into the lorry.

We moved off. The wet clothes made me shiver, so I

stripped down to my shorts. Someone gave me my rucksack, a big chunk of bread and a mess-tin of stew. I made myself comfortable on the rucksack and ate my breakfast. The tin was still hot because they had wrapped it in a sleeping bag. I would take a bite of bread then, holding the mess-tin in both hands, sip from it, trying to time every sip with the jolting of the lorry so as not to burn myself or spill the tasty stew of macaroni and beans. When I had emptied the tin I felt warmer. Someone gave me a cigarette and I lighted up. Now everyone had plenty of cigarettes.

The lads decided to sing, but their songs all tailed off because they didn't know the words. They had grown tired of the songs they did know during the expedition. But it still sounded jolly.

The lorry rushed down the winding road, hooting and braking at the bends. The mountains slowly unfolded and on our left the river showed glittering below a steep drop. It kept narrowing and spreading out again, dividing and flowing together. In the end I grew tired of it.

Suddenly the lorry plunged into the warm, humid air of Kolkhida.

We continued our descent and all the time I was conscious of the nearness of the sea, although it was a long time before it actually became visible.

THE END

Request to Readers

Raduga Publishers would be glad to have your opinion of this book, its translation and design and any suggestions you may have for future publications.

Please send all your comments to 17, Zubovsky Boulevard, Moscow, USSR.